BE THE BEANS

BE THE BEANS

A Parable on the Power of Optimism

Chris Alexander

To order additional copies of this book, contact:
Xlibris Corporation
1-888-795-4274
www.Xlibris.com
Orders@Xlibris.com
128270

CONTENTS

BE THE
BEANS

In today's world and market, there is a tremendous need for individuals who can readily adapt to the challenges of life. In responding to the challenges around them in a way that does not discourage others, these individuals are better positioned to influence the world by making it a better place. We often grow the most when we are forced to experience *pain-motivated change.*

Be the Beans tells the story of a young, frustrated CEO, Jake Carmichael, who finds himself in the middle of the biggest crisis he has ever faced. He has recently been appointed head of LaserTech, a company located in Austin, Texas specializing in digital imaging technology for the defense, medical, and most recently, energy industries. What seemed like a promising future six months ago has turned into the worst nightmare of his life. His company seems to be spiraling out of control with no end in sight. In a chance visit with the company's janitor, Henry Schmidt, Jake learns the story of the *Carrot, Egg, and Coffee Beans* and how his inability to adapt to the challenges around him have stifled not only his success, but the success of his staff and even his relationships at home.

Read the story of Jake's changed life—at work and at home. Explore the meaning contained in the story of *The Beans* and how the spirit of outward focused optimism, combined with an attitude of gratitude, might just change your life as well.

PLANTING SEEDS

Jake Carmichael was one of those young men everyone liked. In high school, he had been that rare combination who excelled at almost everything he did. He was one of the best athletes in school with equal prowess in the classroom. He came from a great family, and most people who knew anything about him thought he was the All-American kid.

During his senior year, his high school physics teacher, Mrs. Krueger, arranged for him to take a trip to meet one of her college friends who was a professor at MIT. From the moment Jake stepped onto the MIT campus, he knew it was the place for him. His stellar SAT scores, along with being valedictorian, made him a shoe-in for admittance.

In March of his senior year Jake received word that he had not only been accepted to MIT, but had also received a full scholarship. Needless to say, he was elated. Based on the recommendations of several high school teachers and friends of his parents, Jake decided to pursue a degree in electrical engineering. MIT had one of the top programs in the country, and the opportunities in electronics and telecommunications seemed limitless.

As he did in high school, Jake excelled in every class he took at MIT. During the summer between his junior and senior years, he served as a co-op student with a start-up electronics firm in San Francisco designing software for businesses looking to take advantage of the emerging computer technology.

He loved the fast-paced environment of a start-up and fully expected to be offered a full-time position the following year after graduation. His senior year flew by, and before he knew it he was back in San Francisco enjoying life as a software engineer, interfacing regularly with people in the electronics group.

From the beginning, Jake's senior managers saw the potential he had to be a leader. They put him on the fast-track, including sending him to numerous leadership training courses around the country. In a company with only 30 people, Jake quickly rose through the ranks, and within 5 years was serving as Vice President of New Technology.

About the same time that Jake was promoted to VP, he attended a party hosted by a college friend who had moved to the Bay area. Jake ran into several friends from MIT who had moved to California. Most of his peers seemed to be doing well, although in comparing his career with theirs, Jake recognized that his career had gone the farthest.

Jake relished the success he had, but never gloated over it because he knew there were too many smart folks in the technology industry to get cocky. As he had always been, he was confident in his abilities, but knew there was no substitute for hard work.

While visiting with one of his friends at the party, he noticed out of the corner of his eye one of the most beautiful girls he had ever seen. They made eye contact and both seemed a bit embarrassed. Jake chuckled to himself as he thought about the fact that he was 27 years old and still acting like an eighth grader who was scared of girls.

He decided to muster up the courage to go over and introduce himself to the mystery girl. "Hi, my name is Jake Carmichael," he said.

She was quick to respond, "Yes, I know who you are. I write for a local magazine, and we've been following some of the technology being developed by your company. I also asked one of my friends if you were who I thought you might be."

Jake smirked wryly and said it was the first time he had ever met anyone who had the slightest interest in his career, at least outside of friends and family. She assured him that she was not a stalker, and Jake was quick to fire back that he would not mind if she was.

Jake found out this beautiful girl's name was Lisa McDonald and that she had grown up in West Texas. She had attended Texas Christian University and had moved to California to work for a small magazine after earning a degree in finance with a minor in journalism. They had an engaging visit, but both knew from the start that something was likely to materialize from their chance meeting.

Over the next several weeks they met regularly for coffee and even had dinner several times. They soon learned that they had common interests in classical music, history, and technology, and they even conversed a bit about politics. They also came from similar family backgrounds and believed strongly in the importance of having strong families.

Within six months it was clear that they were on a crash-course for marriage, and Jake soon proposed. Lisa readily accepted, and the young couple was married by the end of the year. After a whirlwind honeymoon through Europe, they returned to San Francisco to start their new lives together.

Over the next five years Jake continued to pour himself into work. He was internationally recognized as a young visionary who knew how to get things done. By this point he had been out of school for 11 years, and things could not have been going better.

He and Lisa celebrated their fifth anniversary and were expecting baby number three. They already had two beautiful daughters, Ashley and Anna, and all indications pointed to the fact that they were soon to have a baby boy. Jake and Lisa liked the "A" theme for their children's first names, and Aaron seemed like the perfect choice.

On a business trip to Phoenix, Jake ran into Mike Smith, an old college roommate, at the airport. Mike was on his way back to Texas where he was working as a technology developer for HP in Houston. Both of their planes were delayed due to weather, so they took time to visit and catch a bite to eat. As Mike listened to Jake and learned of the success he had achieved since they both left MIT, he had a sly grin on his face.

"Mike, what in the world are you smirking about?" asked Jake.

Mike laughed and said, "I can't tell you how crazy my meeting you today really is. This morning I was talking to my dad, and he told me about this company in Austin, named LaserTech, that's looking for a new CEO.

"They've developed some exciting inspection technologies for the defense and medical industries and are looking for a young superstar to take them to the next level, with a specific emphasis on the energy industry. My dad asked me if I knew anyone who might fit the bill, and I told him I would have to think about it."

Jake laughed and said, "I agree, that really is funny. Mike, I hate to disappoint you, but I have zero desire to leave California. Lisa and I couldn't be happier. Although I hear the people in Texas are great, I'm not sure I want to give up the benefits of living in California."

Mike spent the next 20 minutes talking to Jake about the benefits of being the captain of his own ship and having the opportunity to build a business in the dynamic energy industry. "Jake, at least consider it. The man who owns the company is getting ready to retire, and three venture capital firms are swarming at his doorstep because of the potential they see."

Mike continued, "The owner of LaserTech, Justin Rothwell, is a good friend of my dad's from college. He really wants to avoid selling the company to investors. His idea is to bring in a young CEO over the next several years and gradually move him into a position of authority and transfer the reins over a short, defined period of time. At the same time, Mr. Rothwell would like to sell his shares to the incoming CEO and possibly other senior leaders in the company."

Jake had to admit that the idea of owning his own company was something he had considered at several points in his career, although the thought of initiating a start-up was a bit overwhelming. However, moving into an existing company with a proven track record seemed like the chance of a lifetime for a leader in his thirties.

Mike and Jake looked at their watches and realized that their two hours together had passed much too quickly. They exchanged contact information, and Jake promised to give LaserTech serious consideration. Mike said that he would get in touch with Mr. Rothwell and arrange for a conference call in the next two to three weeks.

As Jake waved goodbye to Mike, he marveled at how the past two hours of his life had seemed to come out of nowhere, changing his preconceived notion of what the future might hold. Seated on the airplane prior to take-off, Jake pulled out a notepad from his briefcase on which to write the "pros" and "cons" for making a move to LaserTech.

It seemed the strongest reasons for staying in California had nothing to do with work, but things like weather, vacations, and friends. In contrast, the idea of moving to Texas, especially Austin, seemed to be attractive in terms of his having the opportunity to really build something on what seemed like a well-established foundation and not have to wait for someone above him to retire before he could be the principal leader in a company.

The big unknown was how Lisa would respond. From time to time Lisa talked about how she missed her family and that their annual trips to Texas never seemed to be long enough. However, he also knew how much Lisa loved the home they had made in California. Jake had been a husband and father long enough to know that there was nothing more important than family, and that included the happiness of his wife.

For the first time in his life Jake was unsure of what the future held. In a strange way, he was ok with that, although he had always prided himself on being one of those people who had every facet of his life planned. Whatever happened, it seemed that a significant leadership opportunity might be in his future.

NEW BEGINNINGS

Right on cue, the phone rang at 9:30 on Tuesday morning. On the other end of the phone was Justin Rothwell, current owner and president of LaserTech.

"Jake, this is Justin Rothwell speaking. How are you doing?"

Jake could tell he was going to like Mr. Rothwell from the start. He had a West Texas accent that seemed to draw you into the conversation and made you feel right at home. "I'm doing great, Mr. Rothwell, and I really appreciate your taking time to call me this morning."

Justin fired back, "Jake, let's cut out that Mr. Rothwell stuff. I appreciate your respect young man, but you can just call me Justin. I already feel old enough. We're pretty informal around here, and I'd just as soon keep it that way."

"No problem, Justin. I'm comfortable with that, and I prefer to avoid formalities unless absolutely necessary. I find it's easier to do business with people I like and trust."

"I couldn't agree with you more, Jake" said Justin. "I know you're busy, and I only have about 30 minutes this morning for us to talk. I would assume after your discussions with Mike that you have had an opportunity to learn more about our company."

Jake confirmed that he had spent time on the Internet doing some research on LaserTech and had even contacted a few colleagues who were familiar with the company. Jake also told Justin that he understood from Mike that LaserTech was interested in finding new leadership to run the company.

Justin responded, "Jake, in a nutshell, I want to find out if you're interested in coming to work with us. I am not one to beat around the bush. Mike speaks very highly of you, and I took the liberty of looking you up. You seem like a pretty sharp cookie and are just the kind of young man we need here at LaserTech."

"I have some great folks around here, but no one I really feel can lead the way I would like. From what I've seen about you, for most of your career you've been leading in some capacity. I have spoken with our senior leaders, and they're comfortable with me bringing in someone from the outside, although they would like input in the selection process. Between you and me, I think most of them are relieved they don't have to lead the company!"

They both laughed and continued their conversation about what the transition plan might look like. Jake shared with Justin that he had talked to Lisa, and they were both excited about the possibility of moving to Texas. Jake also shared that he had been looking into LaserTech and had already started to visit with some of his college friends regarding their thoughts on opportunities for LaserTech's technologies in various industries.

They talked for another 20 minutes on a variety of subjects. "Jake, why don't you and Lisa pick a time in the next two to three weeks and come out to see us? I'm not one to beat around the bush, and from what I've learned today and studied previously, I'm very interested in visiting further with you. I'll set up meetings for you with our senior staff, as well as some of the folks in our manufacturing facility. We have a great group of employees, and I think you're going to like them. Equally important, I think they're going to like you."

Jake thanked Justin for the phone call and told him that he would be in touch regarding possible dates for their meeting. As Jake hung up the phone, part of him wondered what in the world he was getting himself into.

Two weeks before he could not have imagined that he would even be considering a career change. He phoned Lisa, and they picked a time to travel to Texas. Lisa said she could arrange for some friends to watch the children while they were out of town.

The next three weeks flew by faster than Jake could have ever imagined. Jake and Lisa were sitting on the airplane in San Francisco getting ready to take off. Jake looked introspective as he gazed out the window. San Francisco had been very good to him, and there was part of him that felt guilty for even considering leaving.

Lisa could tell Jake was deep in thought and placed her hand in his. They turned and looked at one another. Lisa said, "Honey, I believe in you, and the kids do, too. You're a great husband and father, and we trust in whatever decision you make. I know you're under a lot of pressure, and I just want you to know that you don't have to worry about us because we're behind you one hundred percent."

These were exactly the words Jake needed to hear, and he thought about how much Lisa's support meant to him. He wondered how many men across the country had that kind of unconditional support. He guessed they were few and far between.

He leaned over to kiss her and said, "I love you very, very much. Your confidence means a ton to me. For a long time I have not seen my career as mine, but ours. I know that the long hours that I sometimes work, along with the travel, are difficult for you. I couldn't do what I do without you. Let's have fun on this trip. It's not very often that we're invited to travel halfway across the country to meet with people who actually believe we can help them. I, for one, want to enjoy that!"

They both chuckled and sat back in their seats as the plane moved down the runway to take off. Little did they know, they were soon to be residents of the Lone Star State.

Jake and Lisa landed in Austin, and after collecting their bags, they rented a car and headed toward the hotel. Lisa commented about what a pretty area Austin was and how different it was compared to the western part of the state where she had grown up. They soon checked into their hotel and enjoyed a restful afternoon before getting ready for dinner that evening.

Justin had arranged for the Carmichaels to meet his senior staff and their spouses at a restaurant overlooking Lake Travis. On the way to the restaurant Jake and Lisa both admitted they were a little nervous. As much as they loved being around people, it was somewhat uncomfortable to be among a group of people who knew something about you, although you knew nothing about them.

They soon found that the group's Texas hospitality put all their fears to rest. As they walked into the restaurant, Justin was waiting for them. He was a distinguished gentleman with a thin build, piercing blue eyes, and a smile that would melt the hardest of hearts.

"Jake and Lisa, I can't tell you how good it is to see you both. Welcome to Austin! I trust your travel went well." Justin boomed.

Jake and Lisa looked at each other and smiled—they knew they had nothing to worry about. Justin's wife, Katherine, greeted them both as well, and the two couples walked to a room at the back of the restaurant that overlooked Lake Travis. It was a beautiful view, one that would rival many of the wonderful sites the Carmichaels had seen in California, Jake thought to himself.

All of the senior staff and their spouses from LaserTech were already present. The staff included Rob Evans, VP of Marketing; Mike Cruise, Chief Financial Officer; Colin Jacobs, Chief Technology Officer; Michelle Leads, Director of Human Resources; and Hal Neighbors, Director of Manufacturing. Jake and Lisa also met Justin's administrative assistant, Meg Collins. Justin commented that without her the company would probably fall apart. Everyone laughed in response, although they knew the comment was not made in complete jest.

For the next 15 to 20 minutes, Jake and Lisa chatted with those in attendance who asked questions about their children, life in California, and what they thought about moving to Texas. What amazed Jake was that no one seemed to have the slightest bit of animosity towards him, something unusual when an existing staff is introduced to a new leader from the outside, especially one as young as Jake.

To get dinner started, Justin had everyone find their places at the table. Meg had made place cards to alleviate any confusion about where everyone should sit. Lisa was relieved to see that she was seated next to Jake.

"I'd like to thank all of you for joining us tonight. Of course, one thing I've learned about you folks over the years is that if I have food, you'll all show up!" Justin let out a hearty laugh, accompanied with a few nodding heads. He continued, "The reason we're all here tonight is to welcome Jake and Lisa Carmichael.

"As you know, for the past several years we've discussed my stepping down as president and who would be the right person for the job. Our initial discussions focused on promoting from within, but after seeing everything I've had to put up with, not one of you wanted anything to do with that!" Justin had to stop because the room exploded with laughter.

It was clear to Jake and Lisa that Justin was a wonderful leader and that he had created a warm environment where his senior staff felt completely at ease with him and each other.

"My hope is that Jake will accept this position. He's one of the sharpest young folks in the technology industry, and I'm confident he's going to do a great job with us. Even though he hasn't officially accepted the job, I have a gut feeling he's interested. Let's enjoy our time together this evening and take this opportunity to make Jake and Lisa feel like they're part of the LaserTech family." Everyone clapped as Justin sat down.

The rest of the evening was wonderful. Jake and Lisa thought it couldn't have gone better. There was a lot of kidding among this group, something Jake hadn't observed in the competitive senior leadership of many companies. Even before the next day's meetings, Jake was convinced this was where he was supposed to be.

After coffee and dessert had been served, the group slowly dwindled down to the Rothwells and the Carmichaels. The two couples talked for another hour until it was clear that the restaurant's wait staff was ready to shut down for the evening.

On their way out the door, Katherine grabbed Lisa's arm and said, "Honey, I know this is a big move for you, Jake, and the children. It's not easy picking up roots and moving to a new place, especially halfway across the country. I want you to know we're here for you." Lisa thanked Katherine, and they hugged each other. Justin and Jake shook hands and momentarily discussed plans for the following morning.

On the way back to the hotel, Jake and Lisa didn't say much, but their silence was merely a reflection of their astonishment about how well things had gone that evening.

The next morning Jake showed up at LaserTech's office at 8:45. He was a few minutes early, but didn't want to take any chances of being late. The LaserTech office was nice and functional, although simple in comparison to many of the elaborate office complexes in California.

Justin had previously discussed with Jake that the company had acquired the building, along with 25 acres, to accommodate future expansion. Jake liked the idea of not being landlocked, especially considering that at some point in the future the company would likely need to build additional manufacturing facilities.

Meg welcomed Jake as he walked in the door and told him how much she had enjoyed meeting Lisa. She took Jake back to Justin's office. Justin was on the phone, but motioned for Jake to come in to his office.

After a few minutes, Justin hung up the phone, "Welcome, Jake. I can't tell you how glad I am that this day has finally arrived. I think by the end of the day you're going to be exhausted, but I know you'll enjoy your time with us."

He handed Jake a schedule of the day's activities. Jake could tell he wasn't kidding—it was definitely action-packed. They spent the morning touring the facilities, including the offices and the manufacturing facility. Jake had to admit he was impressed with the orderliness of the operation and how the entire complex had been so well planned. It was obvious that Justin ran a tight ship and knew how to run a business.

What impressed Jake even more than the facilities, were the people. Everyone he met stopped what they were doing and came over to meet him. Although Jake knew that Justin had probably warned the staff about his arrival, Jake sensed a genuine interest from these people and their desire to make him feel welcome. In all of his years in business, Jake had never seen anything like this.

Justin showed Jake some of the new technology they were working on, including some new inspection equipment for the energy industry. "Jake, one thing is for certain. Our national infrastructure is getting old, including part of the energy industry. In particular, our pipelines are getting older."

"My brother lives in Houston and has worked for a gas pipeline company for 35 years. He's had a wonderful career with great people. About five years ago he told me that pipelines are like old people—the older they get, the more maintenance they need!"

Jake and Justin laughed out loud as they both knew this was true. Justin continued. "So, the opportunities that lie before you in the energy industry are mind-boggling. Not only do pipelines need maintenance, but the same is true for power plants, chemical plants, refineries, and even offshore platforms."

"We know more about lasers and how to use them for inspection than anyone in the world. We've proven it in the defense and medical industries, and now it's your turn in the energy industry. To be honest with you, I'm almost envious of the chance you've got. You're going to take this company to a whole different level."

Jake was beginning to feel the weight of the task that awaited him as CEO. It was a combination of excitement, accompanied with a slight sense of fear. To a large extent, it was obvious that this was Justin's vision and company. Following in his shoes was not going to be easy; that was for sure.

By 11:30 AM, all of the senior staff and Meg were in the conference room. Jake was glad that he remembered everyone's name. Lunch had been brought in, and everyone was helping themselves to fajitas. Jake was soon to learn that if he was going to live in Texas, he had better learn to like Mexican food, especially fajitas.

As everyone was seated and started to eat, Justin opened the meeting. "To get things started, I thought we might open our meeting with the promotional video we made last year. I thought it would be a good piece for Jake to see and give him a better perspective on who we are and what we do."

Justin clicked the laptop that sat in front of him, and the video started to play. Jake focused his attention on the screen to learn more about the company. The video was about 15 minutes long and told about how LaserTech had started after World War II when a man, who had returned as a soldier from the war, realized the potential that technology had for improving our national security during the Cold War era.

By the 1980s, the company was renamed LaserTech and began to focus its energy on utilizing laser technology for not only the defense industry, but the medical industry as well. Over the next three decades, the company enjoyed modest growth, but avoided growing at a rate that would prevent them from producing the best quality products their clients could afford.

In 1995, Justin took the helm as president and ushered LaserTech into its greatest levels of expansion, including opening two overseas offices and purchasing the land on which the company currently resided.

A majority of the video was narrated, but the last third or so included an interview with Justin. He explained his vision for the future of the company and complimented the accomplishments of his staff and what they had achieved during his tenure as president.

The end of the video included a closing comment from Justin that resonated with Jake. "At LaserTech, we firmly believe our best days are yet to come. We recognize that the future of our company, as well as other companies in our nation, is dependent upon our ability to attract top talent and keep them inspired to achieve great things. At LaserTech, we're firmly committed to this endeavor and consider it one of our top priorities."

After the video, everyone sat silent for a few moments. Colin, the CTO, was the first to speak. "I really like that video. I think it does a good job describing our company and helping people understand what we're all about." Several nodded their heads in agreement.

Justin asked Jake what he thought of the video. Jake took a few moments to collect his thoughts and then responded, "I liked it in that it accomplished what Colin described. However, I also think the video highlighted a very important ingredient of this company. I recognize that LaserTech has achieved great things from a technological standpoint, but without the people in this room and the other employees of this company, LaserTech is not any different than technology superpowers like Apple, HP, and Microsoft.

"I really liked Justin's comments at the end regarding the need to attract and retain top talent. In today's world that's tough. I think you were wise to recognize that. It is my observation that very few companies today are making staff development a priority, and to their peril I'm afraid."

As Justin listened to Jake, it was clear in his mind that he had picked the right man for the job. He wanted someone who brought his own perspective and ideas to the job, as well as someone who wasn't afraid to share his opinions.

The rest of the afternoon involved brief PowerPoint presentations from all of the senior staff to bring Jake up to speed on the type of work that was done by each group. Jake really liked the presentations and felt that he now had a much better feel for the inner workings of the company.

Jake was not shy about asking questions when he didn't understand something and even made a few suggestions for items they might consider for improving efficiency within the organization. As Jake sat through the presentations, he had to admit that this was the most unique job interview he had ever experienced, bar none.

In spite of the fact that he was the interviewee, he felt more like the staff of LaserTech were trying to sell him on becoming president, than vice versa. Jake found this refreshing and admitted to himself that Justin was the likely reason the interview had been set up this way.

About 3:30 PM, after everyone had completed their presentations, along with some brief discussions, Justin thanked his senior staff and told him that unless they had additional questions for Jake, they were free to go. Jake shook hands with each one of them and told them how much he had enjoyed his time with them.

After all of the staff left, Meg closed the door and left Justin and Jake to talk alone. "What do you think, Jake? Are you ready for this?" Justin asked. Jake had spent the better part of the past three weeks preparing for this question, so he fired away.

"Justin, first thing, I'm very impressed with what I've seen over the past two days. Dinner last night was unbelievable. I can't tell you how much Lisa and I enjoyed our time with you all, especially you and Katherine. In spite of the fact that I just met these people, I feel like I've known them for years. I've always heard about Texas hospitality. Now I know what people mean when they say that.

"The other point I want to address is the sense of loyalty that exists among the senior staff, not only toward you, but toward one another. Our company in California has nothing that even closely resembles this. To a certain extent, I'm convinced about how poor we've been as leaders in my current company when comparing ourselves to what you have done here at LaserTech."

Justin chuckled, "That's because you're seeing the group today. You should have seen us five years ago. We were more dysfunctional than the Griswold family in *Christmas Vacation!*" They both laughed at the thought of that movie, but Justin continued, "Jake, what I realized is that a spirit of harmony and cooperation is essential for a company to be successful. Heck, it's necessary for churches, families, schools, military units—practically any organization involving people with a purpose."

"Jake, hear me on this one; above all else, your job as leader is to protect that harmony, even if it means you have to fire someone. Anyone, or anything, with the potential to disrupt harmony in the company must be dealt with either by forced change or removal."

Jake had never heard such a strong statement made regarding internal cooperation, but he knew Justin was serious. He also knew it was probably the number one reason that LaserTech was functioning so well.

"Happy employees are profitable employees, Jake. It sounds so simple, but very few companies realize this, and even fewer build their companies around this principle. Above all else—keep the peace, my boy!"

For the next hour, Justin and Jake discussed a variety of subjects, including the terms of his employment and the sale of the company. Jake was not completely sure what to expect, but he knew that Justin was not going to just hand over the keys to the kingdom.

Justin posed the question, "Jake, my guess is you have never bought a company. Am I correct?"

Jake wasn't completely sure how to respond, but at this point there was no reason to play games. "Justin, I have to be honest, I've never bought a business or even been significantly involved in the purchase of a business. This is probably no surprise to you.

"However, I want to assure you that I have done my homework. I took the liberty of doing a little research on LaserTech and looking at your revenue and profits over the past five years. I have some friends who are investment bankers, and I've spent a fair amount of time with them getting their thoughts and discussing options based on their perspectives. I have a reasonably good idea what the company is worth, so I guess the real question is what you think and more importantly, what you're going to ask."

Justin paused for a moment. He had to admit he was impressed, but not surprised. "Ok, Jake. Here's the deal. I've spent a lot of time thinking about this. I can assure you that I'm not going to give the farm away in selling LaserTech. We've worked hard to build this business, and I know whoever buys it is going to get a good return on their investment.

"However, I don't want to make the purchase so onerous that it starts the new owner behind the eight ball. So, here's my proposal; I'm going to give you time over the next six months to raise the capital needed to purchase the company. During this time period, I'll continue to run the company.

"You have one job, to raise the needed capital. I can assure you, this will likely be the biggest challenge you've faced in your career. We're in a down economy, and a lot of folks are hesitant to invest in technology. Personally, I wouldn't hesitate to invest in a company like LaserTech, but then again, I have the luxury of having been on the inside of this world for many years.

"I have prepared a list of individuals you're welcome to contact. My gut feeling is that they'll give you half the capital you need. I haven't talked specifics with them, but I have told them I'm planning to sell the company and that you might be contacting them. Whatever they don't invest, you'll need to raise yourself. The good news, based on what you've told me today, is that you have some friends in the investment industry. My guess is they can work with you to raise the additional capital."

Jake sat there for a moment to digest everything that Justin had said. Although he knew that raising capital was going to be part of the process, as Justin presented the plan to him, reality began to hit home. Over the next 30 minutes, Justin and Jake worked out the details. Justin said that he would have his attorney draw up the paperwork and have it sent to Jake the next week.

Jake sat there with a deep look on his face, which prompted Justin to ask him if everything was ok. "Justin, obviously this is a big deal for you and me. For a young guy like me, this is the chance of a lifetime. While I certainly want to do well for myself, in the back of my mind are thoughts about what happens to you in this process.

"In other words, what if I can't raise the required capital in the next six months? You even said that you recognized this was going to be a real challenge. I mean, I don't want to start out being pessimistic, but surely the thought has crossed your mind."

As Jake finished speaking, he was afraid he might have said too much. The last impression he wanted to leave with Justin was incompetence. "Jake, I don't think you need to worry. If I've learned anything in business over the past 30 plus years, it's to concern yourself with the things you can do something about, and don't sweat the rest of it. You've got to think positive.

"The challenge you have before you is something that can be accomplished. Raising capital is something others have done before you, and it will be done again. Envision yourself accomplishing this, and move forward. You can do it."

Justin agreed that he needed to be a little more optimistic and that he would give it all he had. Justin could completely relate to how Jake was feeling, but what he chose not to communicate to Jake was that there was a Plan B if Jake fell short of the goal. However, Justin had been leading young executives long enough to know that you let them fail and then you help them.

Justin knew that Jake needed to learn how to do this by himself; not only in terms of raising the needed capital, but more importantly for the self-confidence he was going to need to run the business. There were times when being CEO could be pretty lonely. Having the resolve to do what it takes was an essential trait that Jake was going to have to muster in himself.

Justin looked at his watch and exclaimed, "Where has the day gone? It's 6:30! I would imagine Lisa is wondering why you haven't called her."

Jake laughed, "I wish that was the case. She got in touch with one of her old college friends, and they went shopping. No telling how much damage they've done to Austin today!" Justin said he knew exactly what he meant as Katherine could shop with the best of them.

Both men stood up and walked toward the door. All of the employees had left for the weekend, so the building was very quiet. "Justin, I can't tell you how much this experience has meant to me. I had some ideas about what the interview process with you might be like, but I had no idea it would be like this. Last night Lisa told me she is ready to move and that this is exactly where we need to be."

Justin was quick to respond, "Jake, she's a smart girl; you should listen to her!" Jake recognized there was a lot of truth in Justin's assessment and said that he heartily agreed.

The two men shook hands, and Justin remarked, "Jake, I'm very excited about this. You and I both know there are so many opportunities in front of you. It won't be without its challenges, but you're in for the ride of your life!"

Justin opened the front door for Jake, and both men walked outside. Jake got in his rental car and headed to the hotel to see if Lisa had returned from her shopping spree. In spite of the challenges ahead of him, Jake was excited in a way that he hadn't been for a long time. He couldn't wait to tell Lisa about the day's events and what was in store for them in the coming months.

INTO THE FRYING PAN

Jake and Lisa flew back to San Francisco, and Jake hit the ground running. He turned in his two week notice with his current employer. Everyone in the office was completely stunned as many had expected Jake to be CEO at some point in the future. Several friends in the company took Jake out to lunch and told him much they admired him and had enjoyed working with him.

Some of the younger staff members dropped by Jake's office as he was packing up and told him they considered him a role model for what was required to have a successful career. On his last day, Jake spent two hours with the current CEO, Mike Worley.

Over lunch, Mike commented to Jake, "I can't tell you how much we're going to miss you. For many of us, you've become the standard bearer for what we expect in our superstars. I have no doubt you're going to be extremely successful at whatever you decide to do, but I want you to know you always have a home with us. I know that coming back is probably not even on your radar screen at this point, but if things don't work out, all you have to do is pick up the phone."

Jake thanked Mike for his encouraging words. All in all, Jake couldn't have asked for a better two weeks. Although he would miss his colleagues and appreciated the opportunities that he had experienced over the past decade, he knew it was time to move on. Most of all, he appreciated how Mike had treated him. Jake committed to himself that in the future whenever a good employee left his company, he was going to make sure they felt appreciated and avoid the feeling of negativity that so often accompanied departures.

Jake knew the sooner he could raise the capital, the sooner he could get started at LaserTech. The thought of starting work as CEO was in and of itself a tremendous motivator to get going with the capital campaign. As Justin had suggested, Jake started with the investor list he had been given.

Within the first several weeks, Jake had raised more than half of the capital he needed to purchase the company. Everything was going as planned, as reflected in his conversation with Tom Sutherby, the last man on Justin's list.

During the course of their phone conversation Tom remarked, "I've wanted to invest in Justin's company for years, but he wouldn't even budge anytime I mentioned it. It seems like everything he's touched turned to gold. He truly has the Midas touch. Justin has many a friend who has marveled at the growth of Laser Tech."

Jake thanked Tom for his confidence in the company and assured him that he wouldn't be disappointed with the return on his investment.

After Jake's conversation with Tom, he spent the rest of the afternoon thinking about his success over the past several weeks. He commented to himself that maybe he had a knack for raising capital. For years, he had heard from others about how hard it was to raise money. He wondered if maybe his ability to effectively communicate and connect with others was the primary contributor to his recent success.

That night after dinner as he and Lisa talked, Jake commented, "Honey, I really think I have a knack for this thing. I mean, for years I've heard others complain about how hard it is to raise capital. From where I stand, it just doesn't seem that hard."

After a few minutes of listening to Jake, Lisa responded, "Jake, you might be right. You've always been a great communicator and have been good at getting others to see your point of view. I don't want to be a discouragement to you, but didn't you mention that you've only raised about half of the money? Before you get too cocky, maybe you should raise the rest of the money. You and I both know that lack of confidence has never been one of your problems!"

Jake snickered and gave Lisa a hug. "You're right. I probably need to guard against being overconfident until I get across the finish line."

Over the next month, Jake started contacting friends and colleagues. Unlike his calls to Justin's contacts, this round of phone calls was not yielding successful results. Jake had compiled a list of 100 people to contact. His approach was to e-mail each person, provide them with a brief description of the company and link to LaserTech's website, and then let the recipient know that he would be contacting them by phone within a week to visit about becoming a potential investor.

Most people were certainly interested in what Jake was doing, including a few who were impressed with the company and future plans; however, very few seemed interested enough to actually become investors. Jake even called Mike Smith, his former roommate and the person responsible for bringing Jake to LaserTech.

"Jake, I'd love to invest, really I would. This just isn't a good time for me. From what you've said, most of the contacts that Justin provided to you are men who have retired and done well financially. What do you think the average age is on your current list?"

Jake commented that he guessed the average age was around 45. Mike continued, "Well, maybe that's your problem. For the guys on your list who do have money, my guess is a lot of them have their own businesses and are primarily interested in investing in their own companies. In contrast, Mr. Rothwell's list likely had men who are 15-20 years older and have money to invest."

Mike suggested that Jake consider adding a more seasoned group to his current calling list, business people with a little more experience, less responsibility, and cash available for investing.

"Mike, I think you have a great point. I'll see what I can do. I have to admit that the points you raised haven't even crossed my mind. I guess I'm too close to the problem to have a very objective stance right now. Hopefully, it will get better!"

Mike offered a few parting words of encouragement. "Jake, do the best you can. You've never done this before. I know it's a new adventure for you, and it feels like an uphill battle, but if anyone can do this, it's you."

Jake thanked Mike for his encouraging words and said he would press on. With renewed vigor, Jake recompiled his list to include several senior level executives and even tried an enhanced networking approach where he went back to the original investors to see if they would provide additional names. Fortunately, he had some success, but not to the degree that he wanted or that was required by Justin for acquiring the company.

In many regards, Jake hit a wall and was undergoing a level of frustration and disappointment he had never experienced before. Previously, whenever Jake met a challenge, he just rallied himself and others around him to accomplish what was placed in front of him.

However, this time it was different. No matter how hard he tried, he just couldn't seem to get others to commit to the investment. Jake was very frustrated by what he saw as an incomplete job.

Lisa tried to be an encouragement. "Jake, maybe you're being too hard on yourself. With Justin's contacts, you raised half of the needed capital, and over the past 5 months you've raised a big percentage of the required amount. Didn't you say yesterday you were at 90%?"

Jake admitted that he was seeing the glass as half empty, but he confided in Lisa that not only did he feel like a failure, but he dreaded calling Justin.

"How can I call Justin and tell him that my best is just not good enough? I mean, seriously, how in the world can the next CEO of LaserTech be so inept that he can't raise enough money to purchase the company?"

Lisa did her best to encourage and console Jake, but she had been married to him long enough to know that he was going to have to work himself out of this situation. She knew better than anyone that Jake was his own worst enemy.

What drove him to success also drove him to a deep sense of frustration whenever he disappointed others or himself. Over time he would be fine, but the next several weeks were not going to be a lot of fun around the Carmichael house.

Six months to the day, a Monday morning in fact, Jake picked up the phone to call Justin. He had a sick feeling in his stomach, similar to the butterflies he had in school before final exams. Although Jake's mood had improved over the past several weeks, he was still very displeased with his lack of success.

The phone rang, and Meg answered. After a few pleasantries, she transferred Jake to Justin.

"Jake, how in the world are you this morning? You've been on my mind a lot lately. What news do you have for me?"

Jake paused for a moment, "Well, Justin, I wish I had better news, but I only raised about 90% of the money that I need to purchase LaserTech. I can't tell you how frustrated I am, but the past four months have been hard beyond description.

"Things started off so well. Your contact list provided about half of what was needed, but with my contacts, I was only able to get another 40%. I really don't know what to say. If I can't do this, maybe this was just not meant to be."

The phone was quiet for what seemed like an eternity to Jake. Then Justin spoke.

"Jake, you're being too hard on yourself. To be honest with you, you got more than I thought you would. I only expected you to get about 60% of the required capital, so 90% actually exceeds my expectations by a pretty good margin. Raising money can be extremely tough, especially when you've never done it before and you don't know the key players in an industry. The fact that you got 90% is actually pretty good."

Jake sat in stunned silence. He couldn't even think of anything to say. Finally, he responded, "Justin, frankly, I'm dumfounded. If I'd known you were going to respond like this I would have been a lot less stressed out over the past several months. I think Lisa was ready to shoot me."

Justin was quick to respond, "Jake, did your being stressed out help at all?" Of course, Jake said no.

"Well, then why do it? Life is too short to worry about things you can't do anything about. Do your best. If things don't work out, start looking for Plan B. Our staff probably gets sick of hearing me say it, but good leaders always have Plan B, and sometimes Plans C and D, if necessary.

"In my lifetime I've seen some of the biggest failures being made by people who stayed on the same path too long. You have to know when to change course. To be honest with you, this was a test. I certainly wanted you to raise as much money as you could because it makes both of our lives easier in the long run, but the main lesson is learning how to deal with adversity."

Jake thought to himself *Well, I guess I failed that test.*

Almost as if reading his mind, Justin commented, "Before you think you're a failure, think again. You not only raised 90% of the money you needed, but you've learned a valuable lesson about doing your best and finding your limits. I can promise you that you're going to continue to find limits in your own life over the next several decades. We all have limits. We just have to be pushed to find them."

Over the next 10-15 minutes Jake and Justin discussed how they were going to move forward. Justin agreed to cover the remaining 10% as an investor and to be subject to the same terms that Jake had made with the other investors.

Jake thanked Justin for his encouragement and for making him feel so at ease with the current situation. It was almost as if the weight of the world had been lifted from Jake's shoulders. Jake just hoped at some point in his career he could bring peace of mind to others who needed encouragement, as Justin had done for him.

The next week Jake flew to Austin to meet with Justin and work out the final details. After several hours of discussions, Jake remarked, "With your permission, Justin, I'd like to review the job offer in detail.

"We'd like to move this summer when the kids are out of school, and I'd like to start the middle of next month. I'll come out during the week to work and fly back on the weekends to be with Lisa and the kids. We're also planning a few family trips out here to Austin to look for a house and get acquainted with the area."

The plan they agreed upon was that Jake would assume the role of president for the next six months, with Justin staying on as CEO. After that time period, Jake would assume the role of President/CEO and Justin would retire.

Jake really liked this arrangement as it gave him time to watch Justin in action, while it also allowed him the opportunity to lead the senior staff and start implementing some new ideas of his own through a gradual transition process.

TRANSITION TIME

The next twelve months seemed to fly by for Jake. Justin had been a wonderful mentor and a great encouragement in helping the senior staff and employees see Jake as their future leader. He never undermined Jake's authority, although he provided useful insights when he felt like Jake needed some coaching. They were a good team, and Jake appreciated the support, especially as he contemplated that in the very near future Justin wouldn't be working with him on a daily basis.

Jake, Lisa, and the children loved being in Austin. They had found a beautiful home in the hills outside of town. It had a huge yard and even had a swimming pool. The cost of real estate in Texas was much more reasonable than what they had experienced in San Francisco.

They were able to sell their home in California for a sizeable profit and use some of that money to purchase the home in Austin. Jake was so pleased to see how his family had adapted. They had made several good friends along their street and even found a church close to home that was filled with many vibrant young families like the Carmichaels. In many regards, Jake knew he was living the American dream.

At work, things couldn't have been better. The staff really seemed to be accepting of Jake's leadership. Justin had been a great help in working through the early stages of the transition.

Jake made a trip to LaserTech's two overseas offices with Justin and was welcomed with open arms. The senior staff met once per week to review the company's activities and address any opportunities and problems that might have arisen in the past week.

Lisa had hired a babysitter for Friday night so that she and Jake could go out to dinner. It had been a while since the two of them had been together without the kids, and Jake had looked forward to their time together all week. They decided to go back to the restaurant where Justin had hosted their "Welcome to Austin" dinner with the senior staff members of LaserTech.

The restaurant had a beautiful view of the area, and the scenery was even more spectacular with the setting sun. They were seated at a table near the window overlooking Lake Travis, and it seemed like the perfect spot to spend the evening.

They ordered drinks and dinner and then discussed the events of the day. Lisa told Jake about some of the things the kids had done and how well she thought they had adapted to life in Austin.

It was obvious that Lisa had made some good friends and felt connected to the community. She had such a warm personality that Jake had never doubted she would adapt quickly to their new environment. He had often commented that some people might not like him because of his driven personality, but that they could not help but like Lisa because of her warmth.

Lisa could tell that Jake had the distant look in his eyes that often accompanied his only half-listening to what she was saying. She knew Jake better than anyone.

"Ok, honey, I feel like I'm talking to a wall here. What's going on in that head of yours?" Lisa quipped, with a beautiful smile that could light up a room.

Jake hesitated as he had told himself that this was not going to be another evening where all he did was talk about work.

"Well, ugh, everything's ok. I really don't want to waste our time together this evening talking about work." Jake knew that was a hollow response and that Lisa would not let him off the hook that easy.

"You and I both know that's not going to work. Look, I know how hard you've been working. The kids and I can sense it. I also know when you're up to something, and I *want* you to talk to me about it. Without your move to LaserTech, we wouldn't be here in Austin.

"You know I'm behind you. I actually love when we talk about what is going on at work. It makes me feel like you value my input. After a long week with screaming and whining children I would talk about anything, even finance and accounting!"

Lisa had given up a good career with one of the big accounting firms, after her short stint as a journalist, to stay home with the kids. She could run circles around Jake when it came to high level accounting, so they both smiled about the inside humor in her comment.

The waiter brought their salads, and Jake took a few minutes to collect his thoughts. He very much valued Lisa's opinion. Although he might have been CEO of LaserTech, he recognized that Lisa's counsel was essential for him to be successful. It had always been that way.

As a leader, there were times when Jake was prone to get down on himself. Lisa had an unbelievable ability to pull him out of his doldrums and provide a perspective that not only made him feel better about himself, but helped him have a more positive outlook on the situation at hand.

Jake started, "Ok, so here's the deal. I've been at LaserTech for more than a year now. Although things are going very well, I realize to a large extent I am riding on the coattails of Justin Rothwell. This might be ok for a brief period of time, but I need to start some initiatives that can be identified as mine.

"All great leaders have vision and are able to rally people to that vision. The trouble is that I'm grappling to find that 'something' I can call my own." Jake stopped talking to let his words sink in with Lisa.

"I completely understand, honey. You didn't move us out here to just have another job. I know you well enough to know that your greatest joy in life is feeling like you're making a difference in people's lives. Some people call that *desire for significance*.

"What's probably bothering you right now is that you feel as if you're in limbo. While you sense some success in being part of a growing organization, you're struggling because you don't yet know enough about LaserTech's capabilities to see where you can go."

Jake was amazed at Lisa's perceptiveness. He had to admit, she had summarized his emotions and thoughts better than he could. He looked at her and smiled, "You're unbelievable. You know me so well, it's almost scary." They both smiled as they knew how true those words really were. Jake continued, "So, what are my options?"

Lisa didn't even hesitate in firing back an answer, "Well, it seems pretty clear to me you don't have a lot of options; however, there are two steps I would recommend. First, you need to be patient. We both know patience is not one of your strong suits.

"You have to give this process time and give the people around you time to build their trust in you. You know as well as I do that good leaders create a spirit of trust in any organization they lead. When people trust you, three things happen.

"First, they're more likely to follow you even if they don't completely understand where you're going. Secondly, they'll give you the benefit of the doubt even if things don't work out at as planned. They realize to a certain extent their success is tied to yours. Finally, and probably most importantly, they will defend you.

"All successful leaders need a group of people around them who rally to their side when things get bad. I'll always be here for you, but as hard as it is for me to say, my support doesn't carry a lot of weight around the office or in the business world. But rest assured, I'll always be behind you one hundred percent, no matter what you do."

Jake was floored. It was if he was hearing a message from a business book on management theory written by one of the nation's top business experts.

"How in the world did you come up with that?" Jake quipped, "I mean, I've probably read a hundred books and articles on management. I'm not sure any one of them ever expressed the need for trust in a leader as well as you just did. Maybe you should be CEO of LaserTech!"

Lisa thought for a moment, "Well, that might not be a bad idea, but I'm not sure you could do *my* job!" Jake knew she was spot on.

There had been more than a few weekends when Lisa went out of town that he was about to pull his hair out by the time Sunday evening rolled around because of the kids. Watching them was often akin to herding cats. He was the first to admit that her job was not only more exhausting than his, but it often lacked the encouragement and fulfillment that his life had as a career professional.

Jake didn't want their conversation to lose focus, so he continued, "Ok, I am tracking with you. I agree one hundred percent with your first step. What's your second step?"

Lisa was not as quick with this response, but she continued, "Well, the second step is a little more difficult because it really comes back to you.

"This is where the vision part of your leadership is going to have to kick in and make things happen. From what you've told me, and from what I've read in the papers, LaserTech is a good company and has provided high quality products and services for many years, but it seems to me the company hasn't had any groundbreaking advances for quite some time.

"I think I even read a statement similar to that in an article on the company you brought home recently. What you need to do will involve one of two things: either develop some new products and services, or find a way to use your existing technology in an industry different from where you're currently focused.

"You and I both know about companies who developed products that struggled until they found the right market. One of my favorite stories is how 3M utilized a less-than-stellar adhesive that some might have considered a failure as the basis for their Post-it notes. It's hard to imagine life without that technology, yet it came from technology that was considered a failure at one point."

As Jake pondered Lisa's words, he knew that once again she was spot on. He made a commitment from that point forward to focus on trying to look for new opportunities in the energy industry where LaserTech technology could be put to work.

Jake and Lisa shifted their discussions away from work and back to life in general. They talked about the kids and how much they enjoyed being parents, but admitted at times that life was exhausting. One of the subjects they discussed was that Jake needed to work harder at *being home when he was home.*

Jake brought up the point that he needed to focus more on the family during times when they were together and not be preoccupied with work 24 hours a day. Lisa agreed and told him there were times when she worried about this issue. He promised he would make a commitment to be more focused on her and the kids when he was at home.

Lisa understood some of the pressures he was under, but they both agreed for his own well-being, it was essential that he have downtime. They both laughed about how kids have a way of bringing life into perspective.

Jake laughed, "Yeah, I took the kids out for a burger last Thursday night, and the biggest topic on their minds was what colors they wanted to use in drawing on the kid's menu."

Lisa agreed, although she admitted that at times it was difficult for her to see the kids as Jake saw them because she was with them all day long. More often than not, Jake was energized by the kids after a long day at work.

They finished dinner and headed back home to relieve the babysitter. By the time they arrived home, the children had been asleep for several hours. As he did every night, Jake went to each of their rooms and checked to make sure that they were tucked in tight, and he kissed them on their foreheads. He took a little more time this evening as he reflected on all he had discussed with Lisa.

He really did love being a father and realized the critical role that he played in each of their lives. While making mistakes at work was not desirable, recovery was always possible. However, at home there was little margin for error. Being a great father was a choice, and he knew that he needed to be more focused on his family.

STRETCHING OUT

Although the defense industry had served as a great resource for growing the company over the past decade, the number of companies competing for a dwindling national defense budget had increased. Unless new initiatives were enacted, Jake could see reduced opportunities for LaserTech's growth in the future. One area he knew to be promising was the energy industry, specifically the oil and gas industry. Justin and other senior leaders at LaserTech had discussed this with him on more than one occasion.

During his time in California, Jake hadn't paid much attention to this industry; however, while living in Texas it was difficult to ignore the powerful affinity Texas had for "big oil", as the rest of the nation put it. Houston was seen by many as the energy capital of the world and was only a couple of hours from Austin. Recent successes with shale gas in Texas and other areas in the country also provided new opportunities for LaserTech.

When Jake returned to work on Monday, he called the senior staff together. He shared with them some of what he and Lisa had discussed the preceding Friday evening. He apologized to them for his lack of engagement and his tendency to push. He promised that over the next several months he was going to focus more on cultivating a strong team and spend more time getting to know each of them personally.

"Heck, with as much time as we spend together, we'd better like one another! We spend more time together during the week than we do with our own families." They all got a kick out of that comment, although a few commented that they needed to not get too carried away with the "touchy feely" stuff.

After the short meeting, everyone went back to work, although his VP Rob Evans stuck around for a few minutes. "Jake, I want you to know we're behind you. I know coming into a new company is not easy. Frankly, none of us felt comfortable leading the company when Justin originally discussed the idea of his stepping down as president.

"I know that sounds crazy. In most companies members of the senior leadership are clamoring for the top position. Around here, I think we all had so much respect for Justin that we realized none of us could follow in his footsteps. I don't say that to discourage you, but to let you know we appreciate your willingness to serve in a capacity that none of us was really willing or wanting to do.

"I also want you to know that we sense your desire to make a name for yourself. This is only natural. My only caution to you is to not push too fast. It will come. As you get to know what we can do together as a company, I think you'll be surprised how adaptable we can be and what we can accomplish together."

Jake was taken aback by Rob's honesty and candor. He responded, "Rob, you didn't have mine and Lisa's table bugged at dinner last Friday, did you?"

Rob let out a hearty laugh, "No, but that might not be a bad idea in the future!"

Jake shared with Rob the tremendous similarities between his comments and the discussions that he and Lisa had last Friday evening. "Rob, I can't tell you how much your encouragement means to me. One of the subjects Lisa and I discussed was trust. I really have no option but to trust you all, but I realize that with my being the new guy you don't necessarily have to trust me."

Rob thought for a moment and then commented, "Well Jake, I'm not sure I see it that way at all. We're connected to you in more ways than one. Our success is connected to your success. If you're successful as a leader, it is much easier for us to be effective in our areas of responsibility. Around here, I think you'll find a deep sense of loyalty.

"Loyalty was a major issue with Justin as he talked often about the importance of our being like a family, especially among senior leadership. He knew that if we conveyed a sense of loyalty among each other that our staff would follow suit. During his tenure there were very few staff issues. It didn't happen very often, but there were a few folks he fired because they were disruptive, disloyal, or negative. Justin had no tolerance for these behaviors, and we knew it.

"What we respected most in him was that he did what he preached. He was willing to fire someone if they posed a threat to our culture. Not many leaders do this. Most leaders are long on promises, but short on delivery. Inner-office harmony is essential and must be guarded at all costs. As you just said, we spend more time together during the week than we do with our own families!" The two men shook hands and agreed that they needed to have more discussions like this in the future.

Although LaserTech continued to have steady growth after Justin left, Jake knew that if the company was going to have sustained long-term success it needed to focus on developing and executing new initiatives. Because LaserTech was widely-recognized as a technology leader and had achieved a certain level of notoriety, over the years several competitors had appeared on the scene.

Although none of the senior staff were overly concerned about the competition, they all knew that to stay ahead of the pack they were going to have to develop new products and services.

Jake became a voracious reader of various trade magazines from the oil and gas industries. He concluded that for LaserTech to enter this market they needed to conduct some market research. They hired a reputable firm that provided LaserTech with an assessment report that included areas for opportunity, keeping in focus LaserTech's core technology strengths.

To gain a better understanding of the opportunities that existed for LaserTech in the energy industry, Jake brought in the market research firm for an all-day meeting to make a presentation to the senior staff.

The afternoon's discussion focused on developing a targeted approach for growing business in the energy industry. This included updates in LaserTech's technology, marketing and advertising efforts. It also included the need to hire a sales staff that would canvass several areas of the country, including Houston and regions of the country where shale gas plays were prevalent, namely Eagle Ford in Texas and Marcellus in New York.

The marketing firm had identified opportunities in the Eagle Ford area as especially promising because of its proximity in Texas and identified that the shale play in this region had a $25 billion dollar impact on the local South Texas economy in a single year. It was hard for the senior staff to not get excited when discussing opportunities of that magnitude!

Everyone in the room was energized and realized they were on the verge of some tremendous opportunities. A quiet voice in Jake's head warned him to be cautious about diving into uncharted territories too quickly, but another voice urged him to charge ahead.

That afternoon and late into the evening, his team crafted a plan for moving forward. Mike Cruise, CFO, outlined a financial plan that allowed the existing investors to be paid back at an accelerated rate over the next two years, but also allowed for expansion capital that was needed for the emerging market opportunities.

The Chief Technology Officer, Colin Jacobs, presented concepts for modifying existing technology for the energy industry, while also discussing ways to minimize impact on their current operations.

At one point towards the end of the meeting Hal Neighbors, Director of Manufacturing, spoke, "I certainly appreciated Colin's presentation and perspective on making sure we do not impact existing commitments. I was starting to wonder if everyone had forgotten about the business that we already have."

It was clear based on Hal's tone that he was irritated, almost as if everyone had forgotten about the role his group played in the company. Several people in the room did their best to help Hal know that he had not been forgotten and that they recognized the important role that his team played.

In addition to dialogue related to manufacturing, a fair portion of the future-focused discussions centered on marketing. In their assessment of LaserTech, the research firm noted the absence of a marketing director. After some discussion, the leadership team decided that Rob Evans, LaserTech's VP of Operations, would head this effort.

The reasons for this selection were obvious to most in the room. Rob had a naturally outgoing personality that made him one of the most popular employees in the company, as well as his being extremely effective with clients. He was often the most vocal among senior leaders in terms of innovative ideas for growing the business.

The latter part of the meeting, and the reason it extended later into the evening, was that the team could not agree on a strategy for selling. On one hand, they agreed it was expensive to hire sales staff with experience and contacts in the oil and gas industry. On the other hand, they all knew that good sales people weren't cheap. Professional sales people would expect a good compensation package that included commissions and bonuses as they helped grow the business.

The group finally agreed to hire at least one full-time sales person, with plans for adding a second in the relatively near future. At least half of the senior leadership had concerns about the costs associated with hiring a sales staff, including CFO Mike Cruise, but in the end, everyone agreed with the proposed plan.

Rob and Jake would start their candidate search the following week. It was agreed that before anyone was hired, each job candidate would meet with the senior staff members individually, as well as meet with the entire group over lunch. During lunch, the prospective employees would present their own business strategy plans for growing LaserTech's business in the energy industry.

Although everyone was tired after a long day's meeting, the spirit of cooperation and unity was exciting. It was clear that the culture of cooperation Justin had started continued as Jake led this group. Jake was excited and could not wait to get home and share with Lisa the events of the day.

Over the next three weeks, Jake and Rob poured over many résumés and talked to at least 50 sales candidates on the phone. After much searching, they settled on a candidate. His name was David Pierce, and he currently lived in Houston and sold products for one of the largest oil field service companies in the world.

David had strong international connections, and over the past three years had focused his energies in the shale gas fields in Texas, Pennsylvania, and New York. He was a Texan by birth, and both Jake and Rob took an immediate liking to him. He was in his mid-thirties and seemed like a committed family man as he and his wife had four children. David was invited to come to Austin for a formal meeting that would involve him making a business plan presentation and also meeting individually with all of LaserTech's senior staff.

After the meeting was arranged, Rob remarked, "You know, Jake, Justin had this saying that used to crack us up. He said, 'Boys, you've got to kiss a lot of frogs, but if you keep on kissin', you'll eventually find yourself a prince.' I can hear him saying it now! I just hope Mr. Pierce is our long-lost prince because I don't think I can take this candidate searching much longer.

"They say finding a job is hard, but I'm not sure it's as hard as finding someone to fill a job."

Jake said he agreed, but commented that he felt very confident in their selection of David. "I really think he's the one. He seems to have a lot of integrity, which is extremely important in sales. We're putting a lot of our trust in him, and to a certain extent, the future of our company is connected to his success."

Jake continued, "Although I'm not overly comfortable with this, I'm not sure we have any choice. I wish I knew more about the oil and gas world, but I just don't. I don't know the key players, which companies do what, and how the whole industry really fits together. David's explanation of the upstream, midstream, and downstream sectors of the energy industry really helped me. I know we're all going to learn a lot over the next several years. It's exciting, but at the same time a little scary."

The following week, one month to the day after the senior leadership's strategy meeting that set the new venture in motion, David Pierce came for the interview. From the minute he walked in the door, everyone liked him. He looked about as sharp as they come. He had played defensive back for the football team at the University of Texas, where he also met his wife.

Both Rob and Jake were excited about their selection of David. He arrived at 9 in the morning and had 30-minute meetings with six of the senior staff before the lunchtime presentation. He fielded questions from the group during lunch and seemed very relaxed. More importantly, he educated the staff on the intricacies of what made the oil and gas markets work.

David also answered questions about which companies had activities in shale gas, as well as addressing questions about international opportunities. He was even asked questions about foreign tax laws, and to everyone's surprise, he had answers for that particular line of questioning.

Although the lunch meeting was only scheduled for one hour, the conversation continued for two and a half hours before Jake decided he needed to rescue David. He could tell David loved every minute of the opportunity to interact, but he and Rob needed to spend time with him alone.

As the other senior staff exited the room, David thanked each of them individually. Jake marveled as he watched David shake their hands at how he had so quickly connected with LaserTech's senior staff. He had never seen anyone in his life so quickly connect with a group of new people. People like David were gifted with this ability.

After getting a cup of coffee, Jake invited David to meet with him and Rob in his office. "David, I have to admit—I'm impressed. I've interviewed a lot of people over the years, and what I've witnessed today is more than unusual. I'm amazed at how quickly you seem to have connected to everyone. Have you always been this way, and I have to ask—what's your secret?"

David was caught somewhat off guard by the question, but answered right on cue. "Jake, I guess as corny as it sounds, I care about people. Don't get me wrong, I love selling, but I also realize that at the end of the day if I sell products without making personal connections, I'm no better than a computer program shipping products from Point A to Point B."

"Early in my career, I was unbelievably driven. I treated every sales lead like it was a play in football, and I treated every competitor like they were the opposing quarterback. From my perspective, games were meant to be won, and opponents were meant to be crushed. My career skyrocketed, and in three years I was the leading salesman in my company. I was outselling some of our guys who had been selling for 25 years and had literally hundreds of contacts around the world.

"I ate, slept, and breathed sales. Everything was going great, and I was on top of the world. My wife, Kate, and I had three beautiful children, and we couldn't have been happier. We were active in church and had a wonderful group of friends in Houston. I traveled a lot, but was able to be home most weekends.

"About five years ago, I started feeling tired and just didn't seem to have much energy. On several occasions, I had severe headaches that left me completely incapacitated for several days. I'm an avid runner, which has always been an important part of my life and helped me maintain my high level of energy, but I even lost the desire to do that.

"After much urging from Kate, I finally went to the doctor. As you might expect, they ran a ton of tests on me. After a lot of poking and prodding, the doctors called us and said they wanted to meet. I even remember exactly where I was sitting in our den when I got off the phone. I must have looked like a ghost as Kate asked me what the doctor had said. I knew it must have been bad for them to want to meet with both of us."

Jake and Rob were completely attentive as they listened to David's story.

"Well, the next morning we went to the doctor. I braced myself for the worst because I expected it to be bad news. My suspicions were correct as the doctor told me that I had a brain tumor. Without going into a lot of detail, it was the reason I had lost much of my energy and was certainly the basis for the severe headaches.

"We were told that the tumor was operable and that they felt comfortable they could remove it via surgery, but that radiation and chemotherapy might be necessary. To be honest with you, at that point I was completely numb. I didn't know what to say as I just sat there in stunned silence.

"I hope neither of you ever have to go through something like that, but needless to say, it changes your perspective on what's important pretty quickly. Over the next six months I went through surgery and a series of treatments involving radiation and chemotherapy. I would never wish that experience on anyone in the world, but it changed my life.

"I had a lot of time to think. The funny thing is I rarely thought about work during that time period. Not that work was unimportant to me, but its importance paled in comparison to Kate and the kids.

"I can't tell you how many hours I laid awake in bed and cringed at the thought of dying. I spent a lot of time praying and I know others were praying for me as well."

David paused for a minute as if he had just realized that he was telling his story to two men who were, for all practical purposes, strangers.

Jake sensed David's discomfort and said the perfect words, "David, please continue. I probably need to hear what you have to say more than you realize. As men, it's easy to lose sight of what's important. All three of us would admit that nothing is more important than our families. Please continue; we're more than attentive." Rob nodded in agreement, and David continued.

"Thanks, Jake. I feel like I'm spilling the beans here, but I really feel comfortable around you both. I want you to know who I am, and this experience changed my life. Well, I can honestly say on more than one occasion I felt like I was going to die. Chemotherapy is brutal and completely incapacitates you.

"I had one friend tell me that the doctors fight cancer by killing everything in you and leaving just enough there to keep you alive. I think he was right. After six months, all of the treatments were done, and I started trying to rebuild my life. This included reconnecting with my responsibilities at work.

"Our company was so gracious, and they allowed me to work at a pace that was comfortable for me. There was never even a hint of dismissal during my illness. The president of the company probably visited me four or five times in the hospital and also came to our home on several occasions. Before I got sick, I knew they valued me for my sales ability, but after that experience I realized they valued me as a friend.

"Within 12 months after the original surgery, I was almost back to normal, at least in terms of my health. I was running again, and our lives resumed their normal pace. However, deep inside me something was very different. I'm not exactly sure how to describe it, other than it's probably best associated with someone who just comes back from war who has faced combat.

"I would imagine that those who have served in combat realize how close they came to death. The little things in life probably don't seem to bother them anymore. Heck, the big things don't seem to bother them because compared to death and never seeing your family and friends again, nothing else really matters.

"One of our senior sales guys, Tim Lightfoot, spent a lot of time with me during my career and encouraged me to redevelop myself as a result of my cancer experience. For years he had warned me about burn out. It had almost become a joke between us—his warning me and me laughing about it. After my cancer experience, he knew he finally had my attention, and he was going to take advantage of it.

"Tim basically became my coach, as I rebuilt my career in a way that was far more balanced and healthy. We discussed three elements required for me to be successful in sales. These are so good I could probably write a book on the subject," teased David. Over the next 15 minutes David proceeded to tell them about the three sales techniques that revolutionized his life—*priorities, patience,* and *perseverance.*

By this point, Jake and Rob both had their pencils out. Although they had expected David to teach them about the oil and gas industry, they hadn't expected him to give them a lesson about living a balanced life.

"So here's how Tim explained the three Ps as he likes to call them. Our **priorities** set everything in motion in our lives. They determine not only if we are in balance, but they determine what defines balance. We must set priorities in business in terms of where we will focus and what we must do, but even those priorities must be framed in relation to our lives and most importantly, our service to our families.

"This was huge for me, and I don't mind telling you—before cancer I never would have listened to Tim when he discussed realigning my priorities, but at this point he had my undivided attention.

"The second P is **patience**. Great sales people are patient. They plant seeds, and they wait. People who I consider poor sales people are all over the place. They never seem to have a plan, and their lack of patience drives everything they do. Great sales people have a plan, and they work their plan. Now, that doesn't mean everything goes their way all of the time, but it does mean they're willing to wait and stick out tough times.

"This is probably more important in sales than any other facet of business. Primarily, because sometimes things just don't come together, no matter how hard we try. There are so many factors that contribute to the success of a sale that are often outside the control of the person doing the selling. These outside factors include timing, competition, and the market's need.

"The third and final P is **perseverance**. When Tim first brought this up, it sounded a lot like patience to me. However, after spending time with him, I realized there were striking differences. Patience is an indicator of how we respond to adversity, whereas perseverance is what we do in response to adversity.

"People who have perseverance press on no matter what the odds. Some of the greatest people in the world are those who persisted against all odds. The great biographies we can read make this clear—success is given to those who persevere.

"One of my favorite quotes is from Albert Einstein who said, 'It is a scale of proportions which makes the bad difficult and the good easy.' I really think that sums it up for me. When I get discouraged, I take a step back and try to put things in perspective and adjust my scale of proportions."

Both Jake and Rob were a bit mesmerized by David. Not only was he an effective communicator, but he had a powerful personal story and an extremely good grip on what was important in life. The three men spent the next 20 minutes discussing the "Three Ps" and how their application reached deep into the core of business.

As the discussion transitioned back to the interview, Jake asked David a series of questions. "David, to say Rob and I are impressed with you is an understatement. You've touched every person you met in this building. I know if you can do that with us, you must be extremely effective in generating business.

"I realize it's getting late in the day, but before you go, I want to ask you two questions. First, why would you leave a good job in Houston and join a much smaller company like ours? Secondly, and I want you to be very candid with me and Rob on this one, do you think you can grow our business with the oil and gas industry? You probably already know this, but there's going to be a lot of pressure on you to make this happen. We're here to help, but at the end of the day, our success as a company is tied to your success."

David pondered Jake's questions for a brief period of time and then responded, "Jake, leaving Houston is not going to be easy. Our family has deep ties and relationships made over the past decade, and I'll be leaving a wonderful company that has seen me through some tough times.

"However, to be honest with you, I need a new challenge. Our company has gotten so big that at times it seems like one person can't make any difference, no matter how much they do. I could literally generate $50 million in sales, and I'm not sure it would even turn any heads these days."

Rob chuckled, if you could generate $50 million for us in the first year, we might just turn the company over to you!"

All three men laughed, as David continued, "So, that's the reason I want to work with you. I want to make a big impact on a smaller footprint. Your second question is obviously a little more difficult.

"Unfortunately, I don't have a crystal ball, so guaranteeing LaserTech's success as a company is difficult. However, I can tell you that there are a tremendous number of opportunities in the oil and gas industry. The key is to identify needs and meet those needs with your technology.

"It's going to take some time, but there's no doubt we will eventually be successful. However, I have to warn you—this isn't going to be easy. Best case scenario, the time frame is 12-18 months; the worst case scenario is probably three to five years. As a company, you have to decide how long you're willing to persevere without generating income from this new venture. If you're hoping for an immediate profit, you're likely to be severely disappointed.

"You wanted my candid response, so you're getting it. I also want to be honest with you because if you have unreasonable expectations, they're going to come back on me. I can handle unreasonable pressures from clients, but I don't want that kind of pressure to come from inside the company. It's not good for you or me. My philosophy is to set reasonable expectations and live with them."

Jake and Rob listened to David's responses. They both commented that they appreciated his candor.

Jake continued their discussion, "Ok David, I like both of your answers as they demonstrate real depth. Obviously, we wouldn't have asked you to come see us if we weren't interested in hiring you.

"We also want you to be successful. It's important that you want to come here for the right reasons. I'm convinced you do. There's no doubt you'll have a significant impact on our company through your success in sales."

For the next hour, the three men discussed the arrangement for David's employment at LaserTech, including various aspects of the compensation package. David seemed pleased with what they presented. Although it was initially less than what he was currently making, he realized the tremendous potential associated with the expected growth of the company.

David also realized that if LaserTech was going to be successful, much of the responsibility for the company's future success rested squarely on his shoulders. He was attracted to that challenge.

"David, we'll definitely be in touch. Before we brought you here, Rob and I made an agreement with our senior staff that we would involve them in whatever decision we made. It's important that we honor that commitment. However, based on what I observed with your interactions during and after lunch, I fully expect you to be an employee of LaserTech."

Jake stood up to shake David's hand, and the three men shared a warm farewell. It was clear they had formed a special bond during the interview around defining and agreeing on what was really important in life.

BOILING WATER

As the senior members walked into the conference room for their weekly meeting, it was clear there was a buzz in the air. David Pierce, who had been hired three months ago, had just been awarded a sizeable project for developing a laser mapping tool for one of the inspection companies in Houston.

In order to meet the demands of the project, the decision that faced the company's leaders today was whether making additional investments would ensure the delivery of the order. The only person who was not excited about David's success was Hal Neighbors, Director of Manufacturing.

"Jake, I hate to burst everyone's bubble, but I don't see any way for us to complete this order in the time period we've been given. You're asking us to do the impossible," Hal commented in response to Jake asking if anyone had any specific topics of discussion to place on the agenda.

Hal's comments definitely brought the energy in the room down, although most of the other leaders knew that Hal was under a lot of pressure these days. Jake knew this was on everyone's mind, so he decided to put Hal's request on top of the list.

"Anyone have any other items they'd like to discuss?" Jake asked.

The only person who spoke was Rob. "Jake, I think we need to table everything else today except for the point Hal just rose. We all know it's the biggest decision facing our company today, and we need to make a decision. We all know Hal and his staff are under a lot of pressure, and we need to help them out." There were nods of agreement with Rob's assessment.

Jake commented to the group, "Ok. I agree with Rob and Hal that we need to address this issue head-on. Hal and I met last week to discuss what is needed to immediately address this issue. We also met with David to try to develop a feel for some of the additional work that might be coming our way.

"Please open the notebook in front of you. The contents provide details on the proposed increases in facilities and staff based on the numbers we've been discussing previously. This is not the first time you've seen these numbers. I would like for you to spend the next ten minutes looking at what you see. Then, I'd like for us to discuss a path forward."

Jake sat down and opened his notebook, making a few marks in the margins to address specific points during his discussion.

After 10 minutes or so, Jake opened the floor for discussion. It was obvious based on the silence in the room that some tension was brewing.

"Well, I'd like to know what you all think," Jake chuckled, "Rob, I remember your making a sarcastic comment about the size of the investment being large enough to fund the military for a third world country." Jake's comment was accompanied with a few smiles that helped lighten some of the tension in the room.

"Jake, I'll speak for what I think others in the room might be thinking. This is a lot of money. I might feel more pressure than most here as the acting CFO, but in the history of our company we've never made this type of investment." It was clear that Mike's comment resonated with more than a few in the room.

To Jake's relief, Rob jumped in to respond. "Mike, I completely understand where you're coming from. You, Jake, and I have been discussing this for a while. At first, I was really opposed to making this level of an investment; however, as I've wrestled through this, I'm convinced we need to make this move.

"Like most of you, I don't like feeling pressured into something; however, I'm afraid that if we don't do something, other companies are going to jump on the opportunity before we do."

Almost as if on cue, Jake continued, "I want to be clear with everyone exactly where the proposed investment dollars are being spent. First, we need to build additional manufacturing facilities."

Hal was the first to agree with that. As Director of Manufacturing, he felt the consequences of space limitations more than anyone.

"Secondly, we need to hire additional staff. While we're not necessarily borrowing money to hire staff, we are making the assumption that additional revenue will be generated to compensate the 10 new employees that Hal has requested. Finally, if we're going to make a big splash in the oil and gas markets, we need to expand our marketing efforts. This includes hiring an assistant to help David, as well as developing marketing pieces, updating our website, and making a promotional video."

"And I want to make one last comment before we open discussion up to the group." Rob chimed in. "As I look through these numbers, they make sense to me. There doesn't seem to be a lot of extra baggage, and I know Mike has done his homework in making sure the numbers are correct.

"We've also spent a lot of time with David. He's probably tired of having to defend his numbers. We all decided to hire David to help us. We need to do what we can to help him maximize his success. I, for one, am very motivated by what I've already seen him do for us."

Over the next hour there was a lot of discussion. Hal and David had to answer numerous questions about the requested money, but everyone remained pretty calm. At the core of the discussion, everyone realized that to be successful as a company they needed to make some investments.

In an ideal world, LaserTech could have used its own capital, but they had all agreed to repay the investors at an accelerated rate. The good news was that in the next three months all of the investment money used to purchase the company from Justin would be paid off.

Jake looked at his watch and realized he needed to bring some closure to the discussion. "Well, to be honest with you, this discussion is better than I thought it might be. I'd like to put this up for a vote. Although I know we don't have to do this because we're not officially acting as a board of directors, we are functioning as the senior leadership of this company, and it's important that we have consensus.

"If we're not all on the same page, we're destined to fail. So, here's the question on the table, are we as a company willing to make the investment required to construct additional facilities, hire more staff for manufacturing and marketing, and generate the proposed marketing materials?

"I have Meg recording meeting minutes today, but do any of you have any objections to the proposed course of action? Not that I don't care about the 'yeses' in the room, but I'm mainly interested in hearing from those of you who might be opposed to these plans."

As Jake looked around the room, no one seemed initially interested in opposing the proposed plan.

"Well, since I started out as the dissenting voice in this entire discussion, I should probably say something," said Mike. "Personally, I don't like the level of risk. But then again, there's a reason I'm the one in charge of watching our money.

"As I've listened to today's discussions, especially comments from Hal and David, I'm not going to be a roadblock. I trust the collective wisdom in this group. I understand that we need to act and that if we do not do so, we risk losing a great opportunity."

Jake had to admit that he was relieved. The last thing he wanted on this subject was a divided leadership team, but at the same time he didn't want everyone just agreeing with what he wanted to do.

"Ok, so will everyone who is in agreement with the proposed plan raise their hands?" Everyone in the room raised their hands. When asked for "nays" from anyone who might disagree with the proposed plan, no one responded. There almost seemed to be a silent sigh of relief by everyone in the room.

During their remaining time together, Jake discussed the plans for the next 12 months. The top priority was to get the construction ball rolling. Fortunately, they had already secured bids, and the prime contractor was ready to start.

Michelle Leads, the company's Director of Human Resources, received also her marching orders for collecting and sorting through résumés for additional staff. Several of the other senior staff agreed to help Michelle, recognizing it was a task that needed input from several departments.

Finally, David was probably the most motivated person in the room. He had clear marching orders to go get more business and the financial backing he needed to make something happen.

For the first time in a while, Jake felt like they had a clear direction for where they were headed. More importantly, he didn't feel as if he was twisting anyone's arms. Most of the positive dialogue had been communicated by others. He realized that involvement precedes commitment. Getting buy-in from other members of the senior staff was essential if LaserTech was going to grow.

CHICKEN OR FEATHERS

It was Thursday evening, and for the fourth straight night Jake was at work after hours. Like the other nights this week, he would probably be there until midnight. Jake stared in disbelief at the numbers that beamed from his computer screen. For the second consecutive month, LaserTech was losing money.

The only comfort Jake took was in knowing that LaserTech's current direction was not something he had created alone; he had support from the senior management. Nevertheless, as CEO he knew had had ultimate responsibility for the success or failure of the company. He was reminded of a quote from John F. Kennedy that was often repeated by his father, "Success has many fathers, but failure is an orphan."

The company's finances had gotten so bad he had been forced to go to the bank earlier in the week to get a line of credit to meet payroll. From what Rob had told him, this was something the company had never had to do previously. After discussing options for more than three hours, he, Mike, and Rob had determined getting a line of credit was the only option.

The only thing worse than a struggling company, was a struggling company with disgruntled employees without paychecks. The only bright spot in the meeting was when Mike asked them if they knew what the difference was between their current situation and the Titanic. After a moment of silence, Mike chuckled and said, "The Titanic had a band!"

They all three laughed and enjoyed a few moments of reprieve from the gravity of the situation. They agreed that none of the other employees could know they had gone to the bank other than the bookkeeper, and since she was part-time, they didn't have to worry about word being spread throughout the company.

Jake was pleased that none of the senior leadership seemed stressed about their lack of progress. He guessed it might be because they trusted the collective wisdom of the group. It seemed natural that David should be under the most pressure as head of sales; however, if anything, David seemed to not be concerned at all.

Like a seasoned hunter, David appeared to be patient in waiting for the right moment to make his move. It was clear that David took the three Ps seriously, especially patience, and applied them to his own life.

David's calm demeanor bothered Jake more than he wanted to admit. In Jake's mind, it seemed like David should be more worried, although everyone recognized that no one in the company was working harder to make success a reality for LaserTech.

Jake also knew that as a leader he was communicating the wrong message to his employees since they could sense his tension. *If they knew the kind of pressures I'm under, they would be more understanding,* Jake thought to himself.

Deep down Jake knew his employees were not the problem, and his being negative was not helping anyone. He admitted to himself that he needed to smile more and help boost morale. Unfortunately, he felt incapable of being the positive influence he knew that he needed to be.

From a business standpoint, the problem seemed crystal clear. The forecasted sales were not coming in at the rate they had originally projected. Sales were increasing, but the rate of growth seemed too slow from Jake's standpoint. With the significant investments in facilities and equipment they had made using borrowed money, as well as hiring additional staff, there was increased pressure to produce.

Although Jake still had confidence that they would be successful in the oil and gas industry, he wondered how much longer they could hold on. David was continually reassuring Jake that he had projects coming, but that it was going to take time.

One of LaserTech's biggest issues was lack of name recognition as few people in the oil and gas industry knew who they were. David said this could be overcome, but once again, it took time. Time was something Jake felt they just didn't have. He had decided that if something did not happen in the next six months, he was going to have to pull the plug. He hadn't communicated this to his senior staff, primarily because he felt they had enough to be worried about in running the business.

Jake sat back in his chair and was startled by a noise outside of his office. He was a little more jumpy than usual for obvious reasons. After a few seconds, he realized it was only the janitor.

Jake had been CEO for quite some time and had probably never said more than 10 words to the janitor, Henry Schmidt. Jake wasn't sure why he had never engaged the janitor in a meaningful discussion since he enjoyed engaging people.

More often than not, when Jake saw Henry it was late in the day and the last thing he wanted to do was strike up a conversation with someone who probably had no idea how much pressure he was under. For some reason, Jake decided tonight was going to be different.

The janitor stuck his head in and said, "Staying late again, huh, Mr. Carmichael?"

Jake sighed and said, "I guess so, Henry. Part of me feels guilty going home when there is so much to do."

"Well, you know, it will always be here tomorrow," Henry said.

Jake quipped, "You've got that right." They spoke for a few more minutes, before Jake finally said, "Henry, you know, I've been working here for more than a year, and I'm sorry we haven't talked before now. Since I took over this job, I've been under a lot of pressure. I know it's no excuse, but I'm sorry for not being friendlier."

After a few seconds of awkward silence, Henry said, "Mr. Carmichael, I know you're a very busy man and you have a lot to do. I can see it on your face. Mr. Rothwell, who was CEO before you, had that same look at times before he left.

"I know you have a lot of pressure on your back, especially with your being so young. When I clean your office, I see the photos of your wife and kids. You have a beautiful family, and I know they miss being with you."

The two men stared at each other. It was obvious that tonight was not going to be like the other nights Jake had stayed late at work.

"Henry, what do you say I order some pizza and we chat for a while? I know you have a little more work to do, and I want to wrap up a few things as well before heading home to Lisa and the kids.

Pizza should get here in about 30 minutes. Would you like to join me in the break room?"

"That sounds great, Mr. Carmichael." Henry said.

"One last thing, Henry, you can call me Jake. Calling me Mr. Carmichael makes me feel older than I'm already feeling these days." They both laughed and went back to work to wrap up the remaining items of the day before meeting in the break room.

The pizza smelled good, and both men were hungry. Jake pulled out a couple of plates and offered Henry a cold drink. As they started to eat, Jake asked Henry, "Henry, if you don't mind me asking, how old are you?"

Henry sat up straight and told him with a gleam in his eye, "I turned 88 last week."

Jake could hardly believe it. He knew Henry was old, but he looked more like he was in his 70s than late 80s. Jake commented to Henry how good he looked and that for him to look as young as he did, he must be doing something right.

As they interacted, Jake found out that Henry had been born in west Texas and had grown up on a ranch. As a young man he spent a lot of time herding cattle and chasing coyotes in the dusty land of west Texas.

Jake commented that before joining LaserTech he had only been to Texas to see his wife's family a few times and that he hadn't considered the places he had seen in Texas something to write home about.

Henry chuckled, "Yeah, I think most people around the country view Texas as a dessert with cattle and oil wells. We used to laugh when that TV show *Dallas* was on the air as it gave folks a funny perspective of what Texas is really like. When I was a kid, Texas really was a good place to grow up, especially west Texas.

"Folks cared about one another. Being a rancher was hard work. Some years were harder than others, but you learned to rely on your friends and pray to the Lord so that he would bring rain during the droughts, as well as protection for your family and the cattle."

"I never quite thought of Texas like that," said Jake.

"Well, it ain't much like that anymore, but it used to be that way. Don't get me wrong. Texas is still a great place to live, and you won't find better people anywhere in the world." Jake had to admit that when they were considering moving to Austin he had found Texans to be some of the friendliest people he had ever met.

Along with Henry, LaserTech had several people who were lifelong Texans. Jake shared with Henry that he expected to be building even stronger ties within Texas as LaserTech realized that to grow their business they were going to have to do more in the energy industry, which was centered in Texas. Henry admitted that many people in Texas, especially those in Houston, claimed they were the energy capital of the world. Jake said he couldn't argue with them as he was learning that to be the case.

"Henry, let's see, if you turned 88 last week that must mean you were born in 1924. Boy, you sure have seen a lot of changes in your life. You were born right before the Depression and have lived through so many technology changes. You must be amazed at where we are today."

Henry chuckled, "Yeah, my grandkids, and now my great-grandkids, give me a hard time about not knowing how to use a computer and not having a cell phone. We didn't even have indoor plumbing when I was a kid. I'm not sure all of this technology stuff is as great as everyone makes it out to be. It seems people spend more time in front of a computer than they do talking to one another. Something about that just ain't right."

Jake had to agree. There were times he wished that he could get away from the technology. Between texting and using e-mail on his phone, it seemed like there was never an opportunity to get away. Even when he, Lisa, and the kids had gone on vacation earlier that year to Disneyland, he had been on the phone far more than he wanted, and certainly more than Lisa liked.

Jake told Henry a little about himself, including where he had grown up, where he had gone to school, and how he had come to arrive at LaserTech. He shared a little about his family, including Lisa and the kids, and how hard it was to be away from them working and traveling so much.

He started to get a little emotional and then decided to change the subject, "I hope you don't mind me asking, Henry, but did you fight in World War II? I've always been interested in that war and the men who served in combat."

Henry was a quiet for a moment and then said that he had fought in the war. "I'm sorry, Henry. I hope my question didn't upset you," said Jake.

"No, no—not at all, Jake. Fighting in World War II was a very important part of my life. A very hard part, but important nonetheless. No one has asked me that question in years, which is why I paused. Even my grandkids don't seem to care."

It seems like most folks don't care about our military and the sacrifices that have been made by both men and women. There aren't many in my generation left. For us, it's part of who we are."

Jake was relieved as he was afraid that he had opened up an old wound for Henry, but it seemed clear that Henry had appreciated his asking.

"Well, since we are on the subject, do you mind telling me how you served? I love history, and I have especially enjoyed studying about World War II. My father and I went to Normandy two summers ago, and I'll never forget that experience for the rest of my life. When I got home I watched *Saving Private Ryan* to help me visualize what those men must have gone through. Henry, thank you for serving our country."

Henry finished his last bit of pizza and leaned back in his chair as if he was going to tell Jake a story he would not soon forget.

"Jake, thank you for asking. It means more to me than you know. I actually flew airplanes in the war. When I was a kid, barnstormers would come through our town and do all kinds of crazy stunts with those biplanes, mainly old Curtiss Jennies. There was nothing like the sound of those planes flying overhead when I was out watching the cattle on our ranch. The pilots would fly low all over town to get folks all excited and riled up.

"The planes would then land outside of town and offer to give plane rides for a nickel. I remember riding into town; I must have been 12, and getting to ride in a plane for the first time. I can still remember the smell and the sounds of the engine as it started. I was hooked from the first time I sat inside a cockpit. I vowed from that point on that I was going to be a pilot, no matter what."

Jake felt like a 10-year old boy listening to the story and probably looked the part to Henry who was more than twice his age. Jake had always loved airplanes, but had never had the opportunity to sit down and talk to someone who flew airplanes in the war.

"Henry, when did you get in, and what did you fly?" Jake asked.

"They started us out in Stearmans and AT-6s. I didn't have to go far from home since Texas, due to its warm climate and excellent year-round flying weather, had a lot of training bases for new pilot recruits. I was assigned to attend flight school in Big Spring, and later went to Tallahassee, Florida for training in the P-51A Mustang. It was a real thrill for us as the performance was so far advanced in comparison to the AT-6 trainers and P-40 Warhawks that were being flown by some of our peers.

"After learning to fly the P-51 including dive bombing, strafing, aerial gunnery, acrobatics, navigation and instrument flying, we were ordered to Boston to ship over to Europe. The time frame was late February 1944. We headed across the Atlantic to Liverpool, England.

"I remember how excited we were to actually be going over to fight. Looking back, it's funny we never even thought about the dangers that were in front of us. We were young, cocky, and invincible—ready to take on the world."

Jake commented, "Henry, it seems like you remember so many details—like it was yesterday."

Henry laughed, "I guess it's all coming back to me. It's been a long time since I've talked about this, but I'm enjoying telling you about it."

"Please continue. This is better than the History Channel!"

Henry laughed and continued. "After a stormy crossing that took about five days, we landed at our port and offloaded to trains for a trip across the English countryside to our ultimate destination, Goxhill, a training facility on the east coast. It was there that we were acquainted with the mighty war bird, the P-51B and where we were trained in the coastal requirements of British Coastal Defenses and uses of the radio systems and the new devices known as radar.

"The facilities at Goxhill, however, had a lot to be desired. Three wooden barracks along with a number of metal fabricated buildings, better known as tin cans, served for living quarters. Typical of the RAF bases of that time, living quarters and mess facilities were 1-2 miles from the hangars and flight operations area. As I remember, after about 6 weeks, we were split into replacement units.

"In my case, ten of us were assigned to the three squadrons of the 357th Fighter Group near the village of Yoxford. We settled into the routine of learning the art of war. They called it Clobber College. We flew local missions for getting to know the area, flying formation, radio protocol, and becoming familiar with weather problems, which were plentiful in the coastal areas of England. Finally, we were given our first mission assignments in May.

"My first mission was on May 21, a Sunday. I remember it like it was yesterday. The squadron was sent to Germany for a fighter sweep. We had a full cloud cover beneath us, so we never were sure of our exact location. We ran into heavy flak over Hanover. It scattered us like a flock of geese, and I wound up with two other guys. We strafed an airfield at Tarnewitz, and I was credited with an enemy aircraft destroyed in front of a hangar. The other two hit aircraft on the tarmac and were probably credited with several destroyed.

"Over the next five months, I had various assignments that included participation in D-Day, Operation Market Garden, and a brief tour in Russia. My last combat tour was on October 15 where a flight of four P-51s escorted a group of B-17s and B-24s to bomb the north coast of Germany.

"All in all, I flew 71 missions that included 270 combat hours. I shot down three enemy aircraft and destroyed numerous box cars, engines, armored vehicles, and trucks. I was awarded the Distinguished Flying Cross, Air Medal with 4 Clusters, 4 major Battle Stars, and several other honors."

Jake continued to be amazed at Henry's ability to remember so many details. He hoped that when he was 88 he could remember half of the details that seemed to come so easily for Henry. "What happened after the war, Henry?" Jake asked.

Henry paused for a moment, as if he was collecting his thoughts. "Well, after my combat tour I finished my time flying back in the States as an instructor. I taught combat tactics while flying the P-47 Republic Thunderbolt in North Carolina. Boy, that plane could fly!

"The war ended in August 1945, and so did my flying career. I was released to inactive status as of September 10, 1945. It's hard to forget that date. I came back to Texas, and received a Bachelor's degree in Electrical Engineering from the A&M College of Texas in 1948. My wife, June, and I were married in May of 1946, while I was still in school."

"Henry, have you ever thought about writing down your life story? At least doing it for your grandkids," Jake remarked.

Henry thought for a moment and responded, "Well, Jake, I know to you it might seem like I did some heroic things, but from my perspective, as well as the boys who served with me, we were just doing what our country needed us to do.

"The hard thing for me to swallow, especially after the war was over, was dealing with the friends I left in Europe who would never come home. It took me many years to come to grips with that. What got me through it all was realizing that I had responsibilities at home, especially after we started having children. My generation knew the value of hard work, and we came back to the U.S. with a resolve to make the world a better place.

"After I got out of A&M, I decided to go into the electronics business, working for Geophysical Service Inc., which later became Texas Instruments in the early 1950s. I worked for them until 1953 when my college roommate from A&M called and said he had an opportunity for me in Austin.

"I drove from Dallas to Austin in June of that year to meet with him. Like me, he had gone into the electronics field and recognized the tremendous opportunities that existed at that time. His idea was to start a firm specializing in designing and manufacturing specialized electronic devices for the defense and oil industries."

"We both recognized that big companies like Texas Instruments were great at mass-producing electronic components, but there was no way for them to effectively develop and manufacture one-off devices and equipment. So, over the next 6 months we convinced our wives that we could make this thing work. June and I sold our home in Dallas and, along with the boys, moved to Austin to start our new venture."

As Jake was about to ask Henry how their company was organized and how successful they were out of the starting gate, his phone rang. He looked down and saw it was Lisa. "Henry, please excuse me for a minute," Jake asked as he picked up the phone. Lisa was just calling to check on him as it was after 10 pm. Jake told Lisa that he would be home shortly and returned his attention to Henry.

"Henry, I can't tell you how much I have enjoyed tonight. You're one of the most engaging men I have ever met. I still can't believe you're 88 years old. Can I make a request?"

Henry replied, "Sure, Jake."

"Ok, Henry, I have a ton of questions I want to ask you about your business. Are you up for our having lunch tomorrow?" Henry agreed, and the two men shook hands.

Henry could tell that his time with Jake had been encouraging to the young CEO. For the first time in a long time, Jake felt energized and excited. He felt the connection with Henry was possibly what he needed to get engaged in growing the business. He and Henry locked up and headed out the door. Jake couldn't wait to get home to tell Lisa about his evening; he just hoped she was still awake by the time he got home.

ROOTS OF THE PROBLEM

Jake arrived at work early the next morning. While at the coffee pot, he shared with several folks his encounter with Henry the night before. Most of them admitted that although they had seen Henry before, only a few of them had ever introduced themselves to him. After hearing Jake's story, most of them were sorry they had been too busy to strike up a conversation with Henry.

Rob commented, "You know Jake, it makes me wonder how often in life we meet people who could really have an impact on our lives, but we're too busy to even notice them. In the end, we all lose. I'm really glad you took the opportunity to speak with Henry. My guess is it won't be your last interaction with him. He probably has a lot of stories. Heck, maybe he could even help us!" Jake had to admit that at this point anything was worth a try.

That morning Jake spent most of his time on the phone calling back people from the previous day. He was meeting Henry for lunch and wanted to be prepared to ask him a few questions that might spark an idea or two that could help LaserTech. Rob's comment about Henry helping the company, although perhaps made in jest, had resonated with Jake. On a piece of paper, Jake wrote down the following questions that he planned to converse with Henry about:

1. What creates success?
2. What prevents success?
3. How can we get others interested in what we are selling?

Jake looked at his watch and realized he had to leave to meet Henry at noon. Henry had invited Jake to meet him at the Old Oaks

Country Club where he was a member. Jake thought it was interesting that a man who was currently serving as a janitor was also a member of one of the more prestigious country clubs in Austin.

Jake pulled up about 10 minutes before noon and was greeted by a young man who introduced himself as Hank. He welcomed Jake to look around the country club, while waiting for "Mr. Schmidt." Hank lit up when Jake mentioned Henry's name, which added to the intrigue of who Henry really was. As Jake walked around, he saw several trophies that had Henry's name engraved on them, indicating he must have been a pretty good golfer in his day.

Jake also saw several photos that appeared to have a young man who looked a lot like Henry alongside several famous dignitaries, including Presidents Dwight D. Eisenhower and Lyndon B. Johnson. As Jake was staring at one of the photos, he heard a familiar voice say, "See anything you like?" Jake turned around and shook Henry's hand.

"Henry, I'm beginning to think there's more to you than meets the eye," replied Jake. Henry laughed as the two men were shown to their table. The waiter seated them at a table that had a beautiful view overlooking the golf course. The waiter took their drink orders and left the two men to talk.

"Henry, I have to ask—how in the world does a man who is a janitor have the resources to be a member of a country club? And the photo of you and LBJ only adds to my confusion. I also checked with HR and found out you've been a janitor for almost 10 years with us and instead of paying you, all of your earnings go to a local non-profit organization benefitting underprivileged kids. What's going on?"

Henry had a mischievous look on his face with a grin from ear to ear. "Well Jake, I figured when I invited you out here for lunch today you would probably wonder what was going on. I have to admit that I'm probably the only person in the history of this country club who ever ended their career as a janitor, although I would imagine a few started out there!" The two laughed out loud as they looked around the room at the other men and women who were enjoying lunch. This was definitely the white collar crowd.

"You remember me telling you about moving to Austin and starting an electronics company with a buddy of mine from A&M?" Jake nodded, so Henry continued. "That was 1953, and over the next decade we enjoyed great success. We have several friends from A&M who went to work for NASA, and they did an excellent job in helping us identify opportunities where we could meet the rapidly expanding needs of the space industry.

"Although I was an engineer, I really loved the business side of what we were doing, including management, marketing, and business development. I traveled a lot in the early days and enjoyed it, other than the required time away from June and the children. By that time we had three children, two boys and one daughter.

"Like you, I remember being pulled between work, home, and church. I really enjoyed being a father and wouldn't trade that time for anything. Some people talk about grandparenting being the best thing in the world, but I'd have to say I loved being a father best. Well, the boys started working in our research and development lab when they were in high school, which would have been in the mid-1960s. They both loved all of the electronics work, and it really was the glory days for many of us.

"The boys followed in their father's footsteps and went to A&M. My daughter went to TCU and got a degree in music. When the boys got out of school, they both went to work for Texas Instruments, which I always thought was ironic. John graduated in 1968, and Michael was the class of '71. I was really proud of them. They were learning a tremendous amount about computer technology, and I was astounded at all they were doing.

"John and Michael both came home with their families for Christmas one year, 1975 as I remember it. The three of us were sitting around the dinner table one night when John asked me what I thought about Michael and him coming to work for me. I had to admit that I liked the idea from the minute he mentioned it.

"I had actually been considering buying out my partner for a while, but was struggling with how I could manage the business all by myself. By that point, we had about 35 employees who were all wonderful, but no one really seemed to want to accept a senior leadership responsibility. That actually worked as it provided places for the boys to serve. Anyway, over the course of the next year, we bought the company, and I renamed it Schmidt & Sons. I have to admit it wasn't a very high tech name, but I liked it and the boys did, too."

As Henry took a break from his story, the waiter came and took their lunch orders. As the night before, Jake was mesmerized by Henry's stories. He was also amazed at how sharp Henry's mind was and the level of detail that he could recall. It was clear that Henry was a very gifted man, and today's story only added to Jake's growing admiration for him.

"So, the boys and I hit the ground running. We divided and conquered the areas of opportunities that we identified. One thing I learned as a pilot that I've never forgotten is you have to look for opportunities and not wait for them to find you! Too many people in business go with the flow. Now, I'll be the first to admit that to a certain extent much of business is responsive; however, to be successful you have to look for opportunities within your market and go after them."

Jake really took that comment to heart, and it was eerily similar to Lisa's comment about how he needed to look for new opportunities for LaserTech. Henry continued, "Over the next 15 years or so we grew our staff to around 150 people and were doing more than $150 million in sales.

"Without John and Michael, there's no way we could have done it. We built a wonderful organization with people who became like family members to us. Like a lot of businesses, we survived a lean year or two, but all in all it was tremendously successful.

"In 1992, we were approached by a group of venture capitalist who were interested in buying the company. At first we rejected the idea, but it began to grow on us. What really attracted us was the size of the offer and the fact that we could give a sizeable cash bonus to every one of our employees based on the proceeds of the company."

We had several employees who had been with us for 30 plus years who walked away millionaires. In general, it was a wonderful experience, and I know our employees appreciated our generosity.

"Several of our hourly employees told us that they were going to be able to send their children to college with the money, something they had only considered a dream. We stayed on with the company for 18 months as we transitioned our leadership responsibilities. The company actually downsized as the venture capital group spun off several of our more successful business units.

"By the end of the day, the core business unit was back down to around 50 people. As a matter of fact, the CEO of this core business was someone you know."

Jake had a puzzled look on his face as there were not many people in Austin that Jake knew other than a few people at church and, of course, the employees of LaserTech. "Who would that be?" Jake replied.

"The gentleman would be none other than Justin Rothwell," said Henry.

Jake almost fell out of his chair. Here he was sitting in front of the man who had actually started the company that became LaserTech. On top of that, a week before he had paid little attention to the man because he'd considered him to only be a janitor.

The waiter brought their lunch, and Jake sat in stunned silence. One major lesson he had learned was that he was never again going to judge someone based on their appearance, or their job for that matter. He had never really considered himself as someone who treated others based on their importance or status, but the recent set of circumstances had convinced him otherwise.

He was convicted in a major way about how wrong he had been about Henry, and convinced that someone with an apparently insignificant job in his company could be someone who had so much to offer.

Were there others at LaserTech who had more to offer the company? As Jake collected himself, he had a few questions for Henry that included what happened after he left, where the boys had gone, and why in the world he had become LaserTech's janitor.

"Jake, the boys obviously did pretty well in the sale of the business. They both took the money they made and started their own investment companies. John became a venture capitalist and has done very well helping numerous small businesses get started and grow. Michael got into real estate and has developed several beautiful neighborhoods in the Austin area. They both spend a lot of time with their families and are both grandfathers now.

"As far as my being a janitor, no one but you knows about who I really am. Over the past two decades, all of our original employees either retired or left the company. I made a deal with Justin that I would come back and clean the office for him, just so I could stay connected. I think he thought I was crazy and probably still does!

"I have to admit, it didn't make a lot of sense when I first came up with the idea, but my wife passed away 10 years ago. Being part of a company that I had a part in starting has been good for me. To a certain extent, LaserTech is like one of my children, or better stated based on how old I am—like one of my grandchildren!" Both men laughed as they thought about how much companies could be like children in that they both required a lot of care and dedication.

"Ok Henry, I have to admit I'm floored. Never in a million years would I have guessed what you shared with me today. I really have come to understand that you have the heart of a servant, which is probably one of the main reasons you've been so successful."

Henry was quick to respond, "Well, Jake, I don't know about that. The good Lord has a lot to do with how successful we all are, but I learned a long time ago that success is 90% perspiration and 10% inspiration. I think a lot of business owners don't realize how hard business really is, which is why so many fail. I don't see that in you. However, one thing I see in you is a great struggle.

"A lot of young CEOs struggle with the magnitude of responsibility that they have. In some regards, it's easier for someone in their 50s and early 60s to lead because they have fewer competing interests like young families and the desire to excel and prove themselves. Older leaders are better equipped to enjoy leading because they see it as a journey, not a destination.

"As a young CEO, you're so focused on wanting to accomplish things that you're not taking time to enjoy the relationships and opportunities you have for helping others. You can change the world through people."

Once again, here was an 88-year-old man telling him the same things that Lisa had told him only a week before. He wondered if they were playing some kind of mind game with him. If they were, it was working.

"Jake, I'd like to share a story I heard years ago that has really helped me refocus on what's important. It's one of those timeless stories that will help give you some perspective on life." Henry proceeded to tell Jake the story.

A young woman went to her mother and told her about her life and how things were so hard for her. She didn't know how she was going to make it and wanted to give up. She was tired of fighting and struggling. It seemed that as one problem was solved, a new one arose. Her mother took her to the kitchen. She filled three pots with water and placed each on a high fire. Soon the pots came to a boil. In the first, she placed carrots, in the second she placed eggs, and in the last she placed ground coffee beans. She let them sit and boil, without saying a word.

In about twenty minutes, she turned off the burners. She fished the carrots out and placed them in a bowl. She then pulled the eggs out and placed them in a bowl. Then she ladled the coffee out and placed it in a bowl.

Turning to her daughter, she asked, "Tell me, what do you see?"

"Carrots, eggs, and coffee," she replied.

She brought her daughter closer and asked her to feel the carrots. She did and noted that they were soft. She then asked her to take an egg and break it. After pulling off the shell, she observed the hard-boiled egg. Finally, the mother asked her daughter to sip the coffee. The daughter smiled as she tasted its rich aroma.

The daughter then asked, "What does it mean, Mother?"

Her mother explained that each of these objects had faced the same adversity—boiling water—but each reacted and responded differently. The carrot went in strong, hard, and unrelenting. However, after being subjected to the boiling water, it softened and became weak. The egg had been fragile. Its thin outer shell had protected its liquid interior. But, after sitting through the boiling water, its inside became hardened. The ground coffee beans were unique, however. After they were in the boiling water, they had changed the water.

"Which are you?" she asked her daughter. "When adversity knocks on your door, how do you respond? Are you a carrot, an egg, or a coffee bean?"

Jake sat there for a moment and pondered the meaning of the story. One thing was for sure, he had little in common with the coffee beans. Life had really gotten the best of him lately and he realized, as Henry had pointed out, that he wasn't really enjoying life and that he found himself on an emotional roller coaster.

"Jake, I can tell you're in deep thought. Don't be too hard on yourself. A lot of life is about perspective. At my stage, I'm just glad to be alive. At your stage of life, an appreciation for being alive doesn't even come into your mind. As CEO, you have an incredible opportunity to impact lives, including the lives of people you will never meet. If your focus is on helping others, it will take the pressure off your desire to accomplish.

"Now don't get me wrong, you're not being paid to walk around, drink coffee, and be a counselor to all of your staff. You're being paid to run a company. However, by providing a vision for your company and helping others accomplish their dreams, you will find that your company will accomplish more than you could ever imagine. On top of that, you'll have more fun and enjoy life."

Jake laughed, "From where I sit, anything is an improvement."

Henry had to agree, "Jake, if you're like the coffee beans, when things are at their worst, you'll get better and change the situation around you. I know you can do this."

Henry and Jake continued lunch, and Henry shared with him more about being the beans and how Jake could actually look forward to adversity as an opportunity to make an impact on the world around him.

When Jake was around Henry, he had an appreciation for every minute they were able to spend together. Part of Jake realized that Henry wouldn't be there forever and that at some point these meetings would no longer be possible. This thought helped Jake put into perspective the events of the past weeks. By the end of lunch, he really was committed to *Be the Beans*!

PERCOLATION

After a couple of weeks, Jake realized he needed more coaching. Even though he was now going home at regular hours and seemed to be worrying less about the company's future, he still felt the need for additional inspiration and encouragement from Henry. He knew with all that Henry had been through, he must have more thoughts to share. He and Henry agreed to meet for dinner one night after work at a local diner.

The waitress seated the two men, and Jake jumped right in, "Henry, in one sense I feel like I have a better view of the world around me, but I don't feel like I'm really having an impact on those around me in the way that I want. In other words, I no longer feel like a carrot or an egg, but I don't quite feel like coffee beans, either. The bottom line is I need some help."

Henry thought for a moment and leaned back in his chair. He knew exactly how Jake felt and had known at some point Jake would need a little more coaching.

"Jake, let me ask you a question," Henry began, sounding like a professor trying to draw the best from his star pupil. "When you read a good book or see a great movie, what is it about the storyline that moves you? I know it might be a tough question, but I think the answer to this question is the answer to your problem."

Jake had a puzzled look on his face and struggled to come up with an answer. Henry decided to help his superstar out a little bit, "Ok Jake, this isn't as hard as it seems. I remember the first time you and I talked, you told me how the movie, *Saving Private Ryan*, had really moved you. What happened in that movie to make you say that?"

This time the light bulb switched on, and Jake exploded with enthusiasm.

"Henry, I think I know where you're headed with this question. There are a couple of things about that movie that moved me. The first was the huge sacrifice those men made when they stormed Omaha beach.

"Against unbelievable odds, they stormed the beachhead and made it through enemy gunfire. There was some level of strategy, but at the core of their success was sheer determination. I found that inspiring. As bad as business will ever be, it will never, ever be as tough as what those men faced."

Henry could tell Jake was on a roll and let him keep firing away. "However, for me there's one scene in that movie that impacted me more than any other. It was at the end of the movie when Captain John Miller, played by Tom Hanks, has been mortally wounded.

"It was tough because by that point in the movie I felt like I knew those guys. It was sad to think that Captain Miller, who had gotten that far in the war and that battle, was never going home. He looks up at Private Ryan and looks directly into his eyes and says, 'James, earn this.'

"At that point in the movie, I lost it, and I'm not ashamed to admit it. As you know, the movie ends as James Ryan is at Normandy with his family many years later as an old man. Standing over Captain Miller's grave, he asks his wife if he has lived a good life. She has this surprised look as if she has no idea what he is talking about, but assures him he has indeed lived a good life."

Jake had to pause for a minute to collect his thoughts. Just playing the movie again in his mind had stirred some deep-seated emotions. Jake looked straight at Henry and said, "Henry, you know what made that movie so moving to me?"

Henry was quick to respond, "I'm listening, professor." They both grinned.

"Boy, have you got that wrong, Professor Schmidt! The moving part of that scene was not what I was watching, but what I was feeling. What Captain Miller said to Private Ryan made me want to be a better man.

"Great stories do more than entertain us; they make us want to be better and change the world. In other words—be coffee beans."

Henry couldn't have been prouder of Jake as he really seemed to be taking all of this to heart.

"Jake, this is exactly what I was looking for. I think you're beginning to understand the value of our little story. The value in a story or lesson is not what we hear, or even what we learn; it's what we do with the story that matters. To change the world, or be the coffee bean, we have to move beyond ourselves and choose to make an impact.

"Your analogy of Private Ryan is perfect because I would imagine through the course of his life, he continued to go back to that experience. Odds are James Ryan would have been a good man anyway after the war; however, like a lot of us, he was a better man because he came back from the war as a mature man ready to make the world a better place.

"I'm convinced this is one of the main reasons our country enjoyed such success in the late 1940s and 1950s. Those of us who were fortunate enough to come back home did so with a passion to make the world a better place."

The waitress came by and asked them if she could get them anything else. Jake could tell she was tired and probably ready to shut down for the night as he and Henry were now the only ones left in the room. He looked at his watch and noticed it was 9:30 pm. Where had the time gone? They both told the waitress they were fine, and Jake asked for the check.

"Jake, before we go I want to show you something." Henry pulled a pen out of his pocket and wrote the letters A C E S on the back side of a napkin. "This has been with me for a long time. As you can see, I wrote down letters that spell ACES. That word means different things to different folks. To pilots it means one thing—success. The best pilots were Aces. I was never able to shoot down five enemy planes, and even to this day, it still bugs me a little."

Henry chuckled as he went back to write more on the napkin. Jake felt like he was in a football game back in high school and the coach was drawing plays on the chalkboard. To the side of each letter, Henry wrote the words Accountability, Commitment, Excellence, and Service.

"Jake, in the war we had this squadron commander, Colonel Jackson. He was tough as nails, and at times we really hated the guy because it seemed like we were never good enough for him. In his opinion, everything we did was sloppy—the way we flew in formation, how we landed, and even how the ground crews maintained our aircraft. He even complained that our barracks were too dirty!

"But one thing was for sure, we knew that Colonel Jackson would make us better pilots through *pain-motivated change*. As crazy as it sounds, I think the fact that we hated him so much actually made us better. One of the guys in our squadron said it was like we were *united against a common enemy*. Anyway, the Colonel had this saying he yelled all the time, '**If you want to be ACES, you have to do ACES.**'"

Jake had a confused look on his face before he blurted out, "Henry, I followed you with the coffee bean story, but I'm struggling with this one. I don't understand how the story of the coffee bean relates to Accountability, Commitment, Excellence, and Service.

"I mean, those are great words and all pretty good in terms of things to do, but I thought that the story about the coffee beans was good enough. All I have to do is determine how to make the world a better place through adversity by being optimistic, right?"

A few minutes before Jake had felt like a superstar as he had cracked Henry's code with the "meaning of books and movies" challenge, but he was struggling with Henry's next lesson.

"Jake, you'll get it, I promise. Here's the deal, you told me a couple of minutes ago that to make an impact you have to do something and not just talk about it. One of my favorite sayings is *speech lies somewhere between thoughts and action and is often a substitute for both*. It is not enough to just talk about doing something; you have to act.

"My question to you is this, what have you done with the story of *the Carrot, Egg, and Coffee Beans?*"

Jake was a little ashamed to admit it, but even though the story had very much changed his outlook on life, he had pretty much kept it to himself. He had told a few folks around the office about it, but not much beyond that.

"Henry, to be honest with you, I've pretty much kept the story to myself. Until now it never really bothered me, but now I feel a little selfish."

Henry could tell Jake was frustrated, but wanted to assure him that things were going to change. "Jake, that's ok. I completely understand, which is why I brought up the ACES concept tonight. As you pointed out earlier, the value in a story is what it compels us to do. ACES will help you do that."

Now Jake was reengaged as he listened to Henry who went back to the napkin and pointed to each letter. "See, the problem you're having is that you haven't given your staff something they can focus on. Even if you were to tell them our story, you would still have to develop some way to engage them in the *power of the story*. ACES will do that for you."

"Just like when I was flying in the war, ACES helped our squadron focus on what we needed to do in order to get better. In our lives as pilots, getting better was the best way to minimize the possibility of our being shot down. Fortunately for you, the stakes aren't that extreme. Your goal is to create a good work environment where people are able to make an impact in the area where you have placed them.

"I can see our waitress looking at us, so I'll make this short and sweet. **Accountability** is what keeps us honest. Knowing that others are depending on us motivates us to do our best. Along the same lines, we must give people permission to kick us in the rear when we fall short. Accountability is the glue that holds every organization together.

"As a leader, your job is to create a culture where the members of your team are accountable to you and one another. No one is an island, and our actions always have consequences that impact others. There is way too much individuality stuff in the world. Successful people and teams realize that they need other people.

"Make sure your people know their responsibilities and that they'll be held accountable to do their job well. Give others permission to hold you accountable as well. It goes a long way to building trust, which is essential for a strong culture.

"**Commitment** is built on trust and mutual cooperation. Look at any great company, team, or organization, and I guarantee that you'll find that a high level of commitment among the individuals within that organization. We are all committed to a lot of things, but organizations must be committed to a mission, which obviously implies that you have one.

"If you don't have a well-defined mission statement, one that everyone understands—you better get one. Everyone in your organization must have a deep-seated commitment to your mission, your organization's purpose, which drives everything you do.

"The next word is **Excellence**. For me as a pilot, excellence meant that I could properly execute my assignment. Excellence doesn't mean that you have to be better than everyone else; it just means you have to do your best. Woody Allen once said that 90% of success was just showing up." They both laughed at that, but also realized there was a lot of truth to it.

Henry continued, "As a leader of LaserTech, you need to challenge your folks to be excellent. This is your number one job as you rally them to be the best they can with the skills and resources they have been given. All successful organizations are good at something, but to be the best you have to be excellent at what you do.

"In today's competitive market, excellence is what distinguishes you from your competition—and equally important—it's what keeps your clients coming back and telling others about you.

"The last word is **Service**. At the core of this word is *serve*. To serve means that you put the needs of others before yourself. Good service is so rare today that when we experience it, we recognize it almost immediately as it stands out from most of the typically poor service that we get.

"People might forget what you say or do, but they'll never forget how you make them feel. As a leader, your attitude should be that you *lead so that you may serve*. There are very few leaders who do this. Most people see servant-leadership as a weakness, but history has shown that to be wrong.

"Two of my favorite presidents of our nation are George Washington and Abraham Lincoln. These two men embodied what it meant to be servant-leaders, and a lot of people, then and now, loved them for it. We need more servant leaders in our world today. I'm convinced you can be that type of leader, if you want to be."

For the second time in one night, Jake felt like a light bulb had illuminated in his head. This time, however, he knew what he needed to do. "Henry, I've got it. The ACES concept is going to help me put into action what I'm supposed to be doing as a coffee bean.

"At our next meeting, I'm going to ask our senior staff three questions in terms of the elements of ACES: how am I doing in each of these areas, how can I personally improve, and how can our team improve our performance."

Henry commented, "Jake, I think this is a great application of ACES and I'd be very surprised if you are not able to get some real traction with your team at this point. Before we go, I want to share one more idea with you."

"Over the years it has been my observation that it is easy to get excited about a new concept, but over time our enthusiasm wanes. I have experienced this and I am sure you have, too. To me this is very frustrating. The best analogy I can think of is our making new year's resolutions to lose weight and exercise, but by mid-March we are back to our old antics. Staying the course is just plain tough."

"At the individual level this is bad, but as a leader it can be disastrous. When you and I get in a "funk", as my wife used to call it, we not only lose the ability to motivate ourselves, but also those around us. In leading you have to find a way to reduce the chances that you lose focus."

Henry could tell that Jake was all ears, so he continued, "So Jake, here's the silver bullet on this one. The key to staying motivated is to get the focus off you and on those around you. One of my sons coined the phrase 'outward focused optimism' a few years ago. I like it because it describes exactly what your leaders should be doing.

"When you are focused on impacting the lives of other people, as opposed to being overly-concerned with your own well-being, good things are going to happen. It is like when you are "in the zone" during a great round of golf—everything just seems to click. It is hard to explain exactly all that you are doing right, but you know based on the results."

As Jake pondered what he had just been told, he remarked, "Henry, as good as everything is you have told me up to this point, I'm inclined to think this is the best advice you have given me. Thinking back, what has gotten me in the most trouble at LaserTech, and probably throughout my life, has been when I have been 'all about me'. It is so easy for us to do."

As Jake and Henry continued to talk, it was clear that Henry's words of wisdom had struck a real chord with Jake. Like a soldier armed with a new round of ammunition, Jake felt energized about the concept of being determined to impact those around him through outward focused optimism.

The waitress came over and brought their ticket. Henry beat Jake to the punch and headed the waitress $100 bill and said, "Honey, you keep the change. We've kept you here long enough tonight. Thank you so much for your patience."

The waitress was surprised, especially considering the check had only been about $25. From the expression on her face, Henry could tell it was probably the best tip she had ever received.

She thanked both of the men and said they were welcome back any time, even if it meant they had to stay late. The two men got up, shook hands, and walked to their cars.

As Jake got in his car to drive home, he wondered what his life would have been like had he not struck up a conversation with Henry that evening so many months before. Needless to say, Jake was glad that he had.

READY TO ROAST

Like a golfer who had just had an enlightened session with his instructor, Jake was ready to head to the tee box. He sent a meeting request to all of the senior staff and was fortunate to find a day within the next two weeks that worked for everyone's schedule.

Jake didn't provide a lot of information about the meeting to his staff, other than the fact that it would be all day and the purpose was to discuss what they needed to do as an organization to get back on track.

As Jake mentally prepared for the meeting, he realized that as a leader he had made some fundamental mistakes that had contributed to LaserTech's current situation. As he often did, he went into his home office late one evening after Lisa and the kids had gone to bed and got out a pad of paper and a pen. Tonight's goal was to zero in on what he had done wrong as a leader. Perhaps if he could figure his own issues, he could share them with the team.

After about 30 minutes of running different scenarios in his mind, he arrived at three mistakes he had made. He listed them on the paper in front of him.

1. Lack of patience in waiting on results.
2. Failure to communicate personal frustration to staff and get their input.
3. Because of items #1 and #2, being incapable of making mid-course corrections as required.

As Jake reviewed the list before him, it all seemed so simple. At the core of all three items was that oft-used word—communication.

How often had he heard in life the importance of communication, yet here he was as the CEO of a struggling company failing to lead by example.

Although in some regards Jake felt like a failure, he reminded himself that failure only occurs when leaders give up. He thought about how failure is a matter of perspective and timing. How many wars were fought where the ultimate victor did not lose a few battles along the way?

There were an almost infinite number of "seeming failure" examples that came to Jake's mind, including the loss of an important football game that seemed to be season-ending, a bad hole in golf, and more importantly, people he had known over the years who turned their lives around after making a huge mistake.

Business was no exception. As Jake thought through the business case histories he had studied over the years, some of the most successful companies in the world had massive failures at some point in their history.

What made the successful companies stand apart from those who disappeared from the radar screen of business history, at least in Jake's mind, was the ability that each company's leaders had to motivate those around them.

These successful leaders helped their companies focus on the potential for success at some point in the future. In other words, Jake realized that he had to help those at LaserTech see what they could become and help create a roadmap for getting them there.

The next week flew by as Jake prepared for the upcoming meeting. With Jake's resolve to get LaserTech back on track, it almost seemed as if things were getting better. David successfully brought in another large project, which relieved some of the stress of their situation, although Jake knew that his own attitude had more to do with his perception of what was going on around him.

Jake was beginning to conclude that attitude had a lot to do with not only being successful, but also defining what constituted the measure of success. Henry's story of the beans ran through his head more than once as he processed the recovery that was transpiring at LaserTech.

The big day finally arrived. Jake showed up a little earlier than usual to go over his presentation for the day. As she always did, Meg had made copies of his presentation the night before for all of the senior leaders. They were stacked neatly on his desk, along with a note from Meg that read, *Thanks for your hard work. I know you can do this.*

Jake realized again how important his attitude was. When he was down and frustrated, it impacted those around them. Worse yet, he realized the impact of his attitude extended to the friends and family of those around him; people he might not have ever met or even known. *Leaders really do have a lot of responsibility*, he thought to himself.

Jake walked into the conference room, and everyone was already there. A few were still getting breakfast and coffee from the buffet in the back of the room. He called the meeting to order, "Okay everyone, let's get started. We have a long day in front of us. I know we would all like to go home at some point tonight!"

To open the meeting, Jake shared with the group some of the struggles he had experienced over the past several months. At first, being that transparent seemed awkward, but after a few minutes he realized it felt good and most importantly, he could tell that everyone in the room appreciated his honesty and candor.

"I have to admit, one of my biggest struggles in life is I'm an 'idealist'. I have a picture in my mind of the way things should be, and when they don't turn out as I would like, I tend to get disappointed. I've realized that my recent actions and attitudes have impacted the direction of this company.

"I'm not asking for a pity party here, but I do need your help. There are a lot of people who depend on those of us in this room. The list is long, but it includes our families, our fellow employees, and even the families of those employees.

"In many regards, those of us seated at this table have the ability to chart our own destiny. I mean, if David wants to make a sale, he spends time with clients and can eventually generate a sale. There are obviously other examples, but that's one of the easiest for us to visualize.

"However, this isn't true for many of our employees; especially for those working in manufacturing. Their livelihood is tied to our success. If we're successful, they're busy. If we're not able to build our business, they risk the chance of losing their jobs even though their performance might have had nothing to do with our failures as a company.

"I'd like for us to focus on spending the next hour going over some concepts that will help us 'connect the dots' for getting LaserTech back on track." Jake went to his presentation on the computer and everyone looked at the printed presentations that he handed to them.

Jake continued, "A couple of weeks ago I stayed up one night trying to identify some of the things I'd done that have impacted my view of not only our company, but also where we currently find ourselves."

On the projection screen in front of him, he presented a list entitled 'Jake's Paralysis by Analysis List.'

1. Lack of patience in waiting on results.
2. Failure to communicate frustration to staff and get their input.
3. Because of items #1 and #2, being incapable of making mid-course corrections as required.

A few of the staff laughed at Jake's title, including Rob who said, "Jake, that's the problem with my golf swing—*paralysis by analysis.* Maybe your list can help me in golf!" He continued, "But on a serious note, I really like your list. Several of us have commented that it seems like we don't get together enough as a leadership team. We all know that when things aren't going well, absence doesn't make the heart grow fonder.

"Justin got us together a lot. There were times when it seemed like overkill, but in retrospect, I think there was a method to his madness. Please don't feel like I'm comparing you to Justin; I've just noticed that our level of communication seems directly related to the amount of time we spend together."

Jake could see several heads nodding, and Mike continued the discussion, "On top of that, I also remember how we used to get together as couples more often. When I first started at LaserTech, my wife didn't look forward to attending the 'The Dreaded Dinners' as she liked to call them.

"But after several years she not only looked forward to them, but they made her more understanding of why I faced some of the pressures that I did. Maybe she looked at some of you and commented to herself, 'Well, at least we aren't as dysfunctional as they are.'"

The room erupted with laughter. Jake was glad to see how much this group seemed to be enjoying their time together, but knew he needed to continue his discussion. "Ok, so here's this idea going through my head. Maybe as a company some of our problem issues are connected to my list.

"As an example, sometimes we have the ability to make things worse than they are because of how we perceive them to be. If I think something is bad, I create an environment where eventually things are bad. It becomes a self-fulfilling prophecy.

"All of you know about Henry Schmidt. To say he's had an impact on my life is an understatement. I wish I had recorded all of our conversations. You all know about the story of the beans, and as a group we've spent time talking about how important our attitudes are to those around us.

"What I've struggled with is how to put the story of the beans into action. In other words, is there some way we can establish a technique that fosters success, while at the same time monitoring our progress?"

Jake shared with the group that several weeks before Henry had shared with him the concept of ACES, which was an acronym for Accountability, Commitment, Excellence, and Service. Jake placed the "ACES" flowchart on the screen for all of the staff to see.

"The basic idea here is to build a framework for monitoring how we're doing as leaders. I'm not so gullible that I believe an idea as simple as ACES is going to turn us around overnight, but I like the idea behind this concept in that it gives us a point of focus. As a minimum, we can build our discussions around each of the four areas."

Jake went to the next slide, titled "ACES Application" that had three questions:

- How am I doing in each of these areas?
- In what ways can I personally improve?
- How can the team I lead improve our performance?

"At each of our weekly staff meetings for the next several months, I'd like for us to spend 30 minutes as a group answering the three questions listed on this slide in relation to ACES."

Jake gave everyone in the room a few minutes to go over the list. He had a way of getting excited about a subject and engaging the audience so that time almost seemed to stop.

"One of the things Henry talked about was that one of his commanders said, 'If you want to be ACES, you have to do ACES.' As might know, in the military ACES are pilots who have shot down five or more enemy airplanes. Henry said it was the goal of every fighter pilot."

Jake could tell based on nodding heads that what he said resonated with most in the group. For some time he had been looking for a concept that could bring focus to their discussions for moving LaserTech forward. From his perspective, it seemed like ACES was going play an important role in that process.

THE BREWING BATTLE

After breaking for lunch, everyone filed back into the conference room. Jake shared with the group that he felt they needed a common theme to bring some coordination and cohesiveness to their efforts in building LaserTech's business. He was convinced ACES was the key. "If it was good enough for Henry and the other pilots in his unit, I really think it could help us at LaserTech."

Jake opened the floor up for discussion. No one seemed ready to dive right in. His unspoken observation was that the number one problem with his team was lack of accountability, with the second being the absence of a spirit of service. He guessed he wasn't the only one feeling that way.

As was often the case, Rob was the first to speak, "Jake, I like ACES. It's easy to understand, easy to remember, and as you said, it sets the framework for open discussions. I think with a little work, we can establish some metrics to make sure we do what we say we'll do."

Colin was the next to jump in. What he liked about ACES was the story behind it. The fact that Henry was a former veteran and fighter pilot who was not only associated with the company, but had also been one of its founders, made the concept even more powerful. Jake admitted to himself that because of his relationship with Henry he had taken all of that for granted.

There were a few nodding heads, although Jake could tell that not everyone was on board. For the most part, the senior staff tended to be positive, which Jake liked. He had always struggled with cynics and spent much of his life trying to avoid them.

Mike surprisingly spoke up with a dissenting commented, "Jake, no offense, but it's going to take more than a good slogan and a motivational story from a WWII vet to turn this company around." It was clear to Jake that he hadn't won Mike over.

Hal also joined in and became caustic. As Director of Manufacturing, he was defensive because he felt as if the group was insinuating that the quality of his team's performance was questionable.

Hal weighed in, "Jake, in the past year we've hired ten new employees. Although Michelle has been a huge help in terms of taking care of all of the human resources stuff, I've been left by myself to integrate these folks into our company. I spend half of my days answering questions that I think should be answered by someone else.

"On top of that, we have developed an entirely new product line for our friends in the oil and gas market. Most of you have no idea all that's involved in developing new products and troubleshooting components when they don't work. To say this has been a nightmare for me personally is an understatement. I probably should have voiced my concerns sooner."

What had seemed like a great discussion a moment before had turned into a train wreck. As was often the case when meetings went south, no one wanted to talk. In some regards, Jake felt like walking out of the meeting; however, once again here was another opportunity for him to *be the beans*.

"Ok, I understand where you're both coming from. Mike, I appreciate your candor and honesty. I admitted to you when we first started this morning that I'm an idealist. I also realize that for you all to buy into this concept you need ownership, some skin in the game.

"I like ACES for all of the reasons we've discussed this morning, but the main reason I like it is because it gets us talking. I would rather us talk and disagree over some points than never talk at all and pretend that everything is ok. I'm glad you feel comfortable enough to share what you're really feeling, even if it means that you disagree with me."

Jake turned to Hal and said, "Hal, I understand some of what you're going through. You and your staff are under a lot of pressure. In many regards, you're the foot soldiers in our company. Everything we do supports what you do. This is one of the reasons that our biggest investment over the past year has been focused on your area.

"I know you're enjoying your new facilities, as well as the additional staff we've brought on board. However, at the same time, it's pretty clear that none of us fully appreciate the stress you're under to produce quality products and also manage a new group of staff. I apologize that we haven't done more to support you."

During the rest of the morning session, Hal shared some of his frustrations. The group listened intently, and several of the staff members had suggestions that seemed to be well-received by Hal. Equally important, the group made a commitment that they would make a concerted effort to walk through the manufacturing facilities at least once per week and interact with Hal's staff.

In Jake's mind, this was the best outcome he could have hoped for in terms of the group rallying around Hal. Everyone realized that they had a fellow leader who was struggling. To some extent, they all felt a little ashamed that they had been so out of touch with what was going on in their own company.

The group continued their discussions during lunch and into the afternoon. Everyone committed that they would take the points from today's meeting and then meet with their direct reports. The idea was to create a company culture built around ACES through constant and directed communication with the senior staff.

FILLING A NEW CUP

In spite of the presumed success of the meeting, over the course of several weeks Hal continued to be hostile and disruptive. Jake began to realize that Hal's comments during their all-day meeting were just the tip of the iceberg. Trouble had been brewing for quite some time. Several of Hal's direct reports communicated to Jake that he had become belligerent and made disparaging comments about both him and the company.

Jake met with Hal three times in as many weeks to discuss some of the points that had been raised by staff members in the manufacturing department, but could never get Hal to admit that he was doing anything wrong. The problems he was facing were always someone else's fault.

After much dialogue with other members of the senior staff, Jake decided to dismiss Hal. As much as he didn't want to have to do it, he realized that Hal had become cancerous and was beginning to infect not only his group, but other parts of the company. Almost as if on cue, Jake remembered Justin's words:

Jake, hear me on this one; above all else, your job as leader is to protect that harmony, even if it means you have to fire someone. Anyone, or anything, with the potential to disrupt harmony in the company must be dealt with either by forced change or removal.

Hal's dismissal had immediate positive effects on the company. The morale in the manufacturing group improved, and several staff members really stepped up and took responsibility. This event reinforced Justin's words to Jake that nothing was more important than harmony in the company.

Within a relatively short period of time, Hal was replaced by Eric Hammond. Eric came from another manufacturing company in the Austin area and was well-recognized as a no-nonsense guy. Several people at LaserTech, including two of the senior staff members, had known Eric for many years. He was well-liked, and those who knew him had confidence in his abilities as a leader.

Hal's dismissal also made some of the other senior staff members take a look at what impact they were having on the company.

During the last all-day staff meeting where Hal had really opened up to the group, Mike had also been very vocal and negative. Most of the staff who had attended that meeting felt he was the one who had been the most cynical and expected that Jake might fire him as well.

In contrast to Hal, Mike realized how damaging his attitude had become. He and Jake went to lunch, and Jake retold him the beans story. Jake recognized that Mike had a tendency to be sarcastic, but encouraged him to be careful with his attitude. Whether or not he liked the story was immaterial. Jake's message to Mike was clear—being positive is a choice.

Jake told Mike that if he couldn't get on board with the rest of the team, as much as Jake didn't want to have to do it, he would be dismissed. Jake told Mike that he would hold him accountable to have a good attitude.

The question on the table was whether Mike could improve his attitude and stay or if he would rather leave LaserTech. Jake gave him the weekend to think about it, but told him that he wanted his decision by Monday morning.

When Jake arrived at work on Monday, he found Mike waiting outside of his office. He invited Mike to get a cup of coffee, and the two sat down in Jake's office for a chat.

Mike apologized to Jake and said he hadn't realized how damaging his attitude had become. He laughed as he told Jake that he had recently seen a poster with the message that read, "Attitudes are contagious, and mine might kill you." That message was an eye opener for Mike. He told Jake that he was now on board and ready to play ball.

"Mike, like you, I spent a lot of this weekend thinking about our current situation. It's become very clear to me that as a senior leadership team we can tackle many obstacles if we're working together, but with disharmony in our group, even the slightest breeze will blow our ship off course."

That afternoon Jake called an all-day staff meeting for the following Tuesday. Each of the teams was to report on their plans for growth. More specifically, they were challenged with making a presentation about how they were going to position themselves for success based on the opportunities that David was bringing to the company through expanded sales.

Finally, Jake wanted to hear about how they were going to integrate ACES into their plans. Underlying all of the discussions, Jake was hoping to see that his modeling a positive attitude would have an effect on the leadership of his senior staff members. He was really beginning to believe that success had more to do with attitude than with what was actually accomplished.

Prior to the following week's staff meeting, Jake had individual meetings with all of the leadership team members. To achieve a greater level of accountability, he wanted each group to start reporting on activities in their respective groups, with a specific emphasis on ACES. Each group would be given five minutes, as Jake was cognizant of the tendency that some had for being a little long winded.

Rob Evans, VP, would report on the overall health of the company and observations from senior management. Mike Cruise would report on the financial status on the company as acting CFO. Colin Jacobs would report on the technology outlook as the company's Chief Technology Officer. Eric Hammond would discuss what was taking place in manufacturing. Michelle Leads would discuss personnel issues as head of Human Resources. Finally, David Pierce, Head of Sales, would provide information to the group on emerging opportunities.

Tuesday morning arrived, and Jake was pleased to see that everyone was on time. Fortunately, during his tenure as CEO he had never had a problem with staff members not being on time to meetings. It was clear that his leaders were busy and valued not only their time, but the time of their fellow employees. Jake also guessed that Justin might have been a stickler for punctuality.

Jake kicked the meeting off and said that after some opening comments, they were going to spend the first 30 minutes focused on their ACES discussions. His opening remarks focused mainly on how pleased he was to see how all of the groups were working together.

He emphasized, as he had done previously, how important their getting along was to the success of the company. He chuckled, "Our getting along is no guarantee of success, but being dysfunctional is almost a sure-fire way to fail."

As much as some members of the group didn't want to admit it, ACES actually brought focus to their discussion. There were several times during the meeting when comments from one group leader sparked ideas from another group.

Through these discussions, the group realized how they could work together. One group's weakness in accountability was met by another group's strength. By building bridges between groups, they started to understand that as an organization there were very few things they could not accomplish.

The highlight of the day's conversation centered on how to best engage employees. LaserTech was fortunate to have senior leaders that were naturally inclined to take charge of their areas of responsibility. The same could not be same of many of the mid-level managers and hourly employees, who seemed to have little interest in making decisions. These staff members wanted to be told what to do.

"You know, there have been a lot of studies on this particular issue," Michelle chimed in. "In general, we expect hourly employees to be followers. The last thing we want are 100 people doing whatever they want to do. What we're experiencing is typical and to be expected."

The group agreed with Michelle, although several of the senior leaders wished their mid-level managers would "step it up" as Colin suggested.

As the new person on the block, Eric Hammond decided to throw in his opinion. "When I first started here at LaserTech I struggled with this particular issue, but I recently identified a pretty good solution that has been working well. I took our four mid-level managers out to lunch. Other than just wanting to spend time with them and get to know them personally, I had two ulterior motives. The first was to get their opinion on what was working and what wasn't. They were very candid and had some excellent ideas.

"My second motive was to get their commitment to an idea I wanted to roll out. I shared with them that I thought they should be given more responsibility to lead the group. Obviously, they know more about the company than I do, so there was little debate on their part regarding experience. However, I knew I needed to convince them they could help each other be successful."

Eric shared with the senior staff members, as he had with his four mid-level managers during lunch, his solution for solving the leadership dilemma. He decided that each manager would be responsible for leading the team one week per month, something he called distributed leadership. Recognizing that each manager's term would eventually come up, Eric helped his managers understand the importance of working together.

Almost overnight the problems went away, reported Eric. He told the group his technique was borrowed from his experience in attending the Army's Officer Basic Course. His philosophy was that if it was good enough for the U.S. Army, it was good enough for LaserTech.

It was amazing to see the room light up as Eric shared his story with the group. Almost immediately Jake could see the gears turning in the heads of his other senior leaders. Eric agreed that during next week's staff meeting he would share the basic principles associated with his mid-level leadership program, based on a tried and true method of achieving accountability in a group through *distributed leadership*, as he liked to call it.

Jake had a few closing comments before dismissing the group. He thanked them for their time and asked them to contact him if they had any additional ideas or thoughts. Through all of the recent experiences, including firing Hal and making a believer out of Mike, Jake's confidence as a leader had grown significantly. In his mind, this meeting was a reflection that he was doing something correctly. After so many months of experiencing limited positive emotions, it was a good feeling.

Interestingly enough, over the next quarter LaserTech's profits surged. It seemed clear to the senior staff that the spirit of cooperation brought about by their open discussions, facilitated by the ACES dialogue, contributed greatly to their recent success. Jake wondered how many problems in other struggling companies had more to do with what is going on inside the company and less with external situations and circumstances.

JUBILANT JAVA

After the ups and downs of the last year, Jake decided that he and Lisa needed a little rest and relaxation. Lisa's parents agreed to watch the children while they took a trip to Colorado for some skiing and mountain fresh air.

They flew into Denver and drove west towards the Rockies. Jake had made several trips to Denver during the winter months, and it always amazed him how within a single hour he could go from the flatlands around Denver's airport to the majestic snowy peaks of the Rockies.

He and Lisa checked into the condo and unpacked their bags. Tomorrow they would ski, but tonight was an opportunity to visit and unwind. Lisa assumed it would take Jake a couple of days to unwind; it always did. However, she would soon learn that this time would be different.

Jake was lying on the bed looking out the window, and Lisa asked him if he was going to check in with the office and at least look at his phone to retrieve e-mails.

"No, we've got people at the office who can do that. I told them to call me if they needed anything, but only if absolutely necessary. I told them I really needed some time away to unwind."

Lisa stopped what she was doing as she couldn't believe what she was hearing. This had never happened in the history of their marriage. There was always something that required Jake's attention. "Jake, you didn't resign, did you?" Lisa said, only half-joking. "I mean, this is so unlike you."

Jake responded, "Maybe it's not like the 'old me', but after the experiences over the past year I think that 'Jake' might just be gone for good. A lot has happened to help me refocus on what's important. At the same time, after last month's explosion with the staff, I decided I needed to develop a greater level of trust in their abilities. It's very clear to me that they appreciate that trust.

"The last time Henry and I were together he asked me a very pointed question, 'Jake, as you look back over this entire experience over the past two years in seeing the company turn around—what have you learned?' As scary as it sounds, I had a very direct answer for him; almost as if I had prepared for that moment.

"I told him that if I had to do it all over again, I'd only change one thing, and that's my perspective. I've learned that success often takes longer than we originally anticipate, but failure is never as close as we imagine it to be. I could tell he really liked that, and personally, I did, too!"

Jake and Lisa decided to go out to dinner. Lisa looked on the Internet and found a nice restaurant that promised a beautiful view of the mountains. Upon arriving at the restaurant, they both admitted they were not disappointed. The restaurant and view were everything the website had promised they would be. Much like their dinner in Austin so many months ago, they both knew that tonight's discussion was going to be important in their moving forward.

"Lisa, you know, Henry has really had an impact on my life. It's hard to imagine where I would be now had he not entered the picture. As much as his encouragement and advice have helped me at work, I feel like we need to do more. I mean you and me.

"We've both been blessed beyond anything we could ever have dreamed 20 years ago. At times I feel guilty for all that we have, especially when they are so many hurting people in the world. If LaserTech grows as I think it might, all of our employees are going to benefit. So, here's my question to you, how can we take what we've been given financially and help other people?"

Jake sat there for a moment and gave Lisa a few minutes to collect her thoughts. "You know, Jake, it's almost scary, but I know exactly who we need help. Several weeks ago a friend of mine, Marcy Irvine, called me about a friend of hers who recently lost her husband to cancer. The lady's name is Carrie Schneider. She has two children, an 11-year old son and a daughter who's 7.

"I can't even imagine what that family is going through. They had to move in with her parents, and she's looking for a job. Can you imagine our children without you? That little boy and little girl are going to have an uphill battle.

"There's no doubt that we can help them out financially, but I'd like for us to do even more. Jake, you're such a good dad, and I know how much you love our kids. What if this family was brought to our attention for a reason?"

Once again, Jake was amazed at how quickly Lisa responded to his request. "Let's do it, Lisa. I mean seriously, let's not just talk about it, but let's make an investment in this family. When we get home, I'd like for you to get in touch with Carrie. Let's have them over for dinner and start building a relationship with her and the kids. Also, try to find out something about her background, and I'll see what I can do to help her find a job."

As was often the case, Lisa had a way of motivating Jake. More importantly, she was motivating him to make investments of his skills and resources outside of work. Both Jake and Lisa had bought into the idea of *being the beans*, and the opportunity to make an impact on the Schneider family seemed like a great way to put words into action.

Lisa and Jake finished up dinner and headed back to the condo. They were both exhausted and knew they needed to get some rest before a long day of skiing.

The next several days in Colorado were wonderful. Jake and Lisa had both grown up skiing, and even though neither of them had been in several years, it was not long before they were back in their old form. Skiing had a way of bringing out the daredevil in Jake, and Lisa doubled over in laughter on more than one occasion as Jake tried to relive the glory days of his youth. They both concluded he was no longer 20, and he now had a few bruises to prove it.

After three days of skiing, both Jake and Lisa were ready to get home. Although they missed the children, Lisa's biggest concern was that Jake might wind up breaking a leg or hitting a tree if he kept up the same pace. Jake agreed that he should probably stop before something happened that they would both regret.

As Jake finished packing up the car before heading back to Denver, he took a moment to look at the mountains and enjoy the view before returning back to Texas. As pretty as Austin was with its rolling hills, nothing compared to the Rockies.

As Jake thought back to work and LaserTech, he knew that a mountain range of opportunities lay before him and the other leaders at LaserTech; however, he had confidence his team could conquer the mountain of challenges in their future.

During their drive back to Denver, Jake and Lisa talked about the Schneiders and some of the ways that could impact this hurting family. They committed to doing whatever they could to ensure that the Schneider children would have the same opportunities that their own children would have.

BARISTA'S BREW

Jake looked outside his office through the window that offered a beautiful view of the hills outside Austin. He thought about the great time he had last weekend in the mountains of Colorado with Lisa. He marveled at how much his perspective had changed. He truly was a changed man after having put ACES to work as a leader at LaserTech and *being the beans* in his personal life through outward focused optimism.

It was hard to believe how much his life had transformed over the past year. Six months ago everything seemed to be a mess with no chance of things getting better. Now, life couldn't be better. His trip to Colorado with Lisa had been just what the doctor ordered. He felt rejuvenated and re-engaged in getting LaserTech on the map.

When people asked how he was doing, he was quick to say—*living the dream by being the beans.* As crazy and funny as it sounded, he really meant it. He even had T-shirts made for the employees, and they had recently worn them while working on a local Habitat for Humanity project.

Needless to say, during the work project his staff had a lot of opportunities to share the story of the *Carrot, Egg, and Coffee Beans* to people who asked about their T-shirts.

Although LaserTech was still not completely where Jake and the senior staff wanted it to be, Jake realized that the size of a problem is defined by how one views the problem, not how big it really is. He was reminded of the Albert Einstein quote that David had provided to Rob and him during his interview: *It is a scale of proportions which makes the bad difficult and the good easy.*

As Jake was staring out the window, the phone rang. He leaned over and noticed the caller ID showed a familiar number, "Good morning, Henry. Yes, it has been a while. Oh, you heard about the T-shirts? That's hilarious. Yeah, we even got mentioned in the paper with a group photo of us in our *Living the dream by being the beans* T-shirts. Our team has definitely got the story down by now. Yes, actually, I am available for lunch today. I'll see you at the club at noon. Take care, see you then."

A little before noon Jake headed to the country club to meet Henry and realized he felt like a fourth grader who had completed his homework and was ready to turn in his assignment to the teacher. Since his last meeting with Henry, he had fully developed the concept behind ACES, as well as helping his employees embrace the idea of *being the beans* by maintaining a positive attitude.

One of the advantages in being CEO was the opportunity to influence his staff in a way that would not have been possible had he not been in the senior leadership position. He realized that his serving in this capacity was not only a great privilege, but also a responsibility in that he needed to be a servant-leader. He also thought about the notion that he was Henry's "business grandson". He certainly felt a sense of pride in that.

Henry arrived right on time, as usual, and the two men were seated for lunch. Jake pulled out a piece of paper and handed it to Henry. Henry spent a few minutes looking at the paper and felt a tremendous sense of pride in what he saw.

"Jake, this is really good. You've taken ACES to a whole new level, like I knew you would! My guess is that you've shared this with your staff and helped them understand how both individually and corporately putting ACES to work can really transform a company."

Jake spent the next few minutes going over the diagram with Henry and highlighting some of the finer points. He explained that the simple diagram allowed him to easily present ACES as a process and how each stage was extremely important in ensuring the success of the subsequent stage.

Accountability
Set clear expectations

Commitment
Carry out the mission at all costs

Excellence
DO over SHOW ratio > 1

Service
Expectations + 1

As Henry looked at the chart, he told Jake, "I really like it, and I can see you have introduced a little math into the presentation. This is just what I would expect from an engineer!"

They both laughed, and Jake went on to explain, "Yes, that was an idea one of our guys came up with, and I thought it was really good. I could spend a lot of time on the last two blocks, but here are my thoughts in a nutshell.

"First is the 'DO over SHOW ratio being greater than 1'. A lot of people talk about the importance of providing quality services and goods, but most companies tend to over-promise and under-deliver. We don't want to do that. We want LaserTech clients to see that what we deliver is at least as good as what we've communicated they will get, but we never want that ratio to be less than 1."

Henry thought about that for a moment, "I like it. It's simple enough for a fourth grader to understand, but significant enough to transform a company!"

Jake continued, "The next equation is 'Expectations + 1'. It somewhat goes hand-in-hand with the DO over SHOW ratio being greater than 1, but it's more focused. There are times when clients demand that we do more than what we've committed. Also, there are times when we place these demands on ourselves. As good as that might sound, it can be dangerous.

"When we continually strive to do more and more for one client, it means we have to sacrifice quality for another. At first it sounds like not being focused on exceeding client expectations is bad; however, we're convinced it's not. We've concluded that it's better to offer consistently good service than offer super over-the-top service to one or two clients, while sacrificing what we do for others.

"To be honest with you, I think this issue has been an ongoing problem at LaserTech for some time—trying to keep a few clients happy at the expense of disappointing others. We've had several clients who have demanded so much of us that we dropped the ball with others. In moving into the energy industry, with new clients, we knew that we couldn't afford to do this.

"At first it was a little difficult as we had to sit down with several clients and explain to them that things needed to change and that we felt their demands were disproportionate with our compensation.

We told them that we needed to achieve a balance between what they expected from us and what we could deliver.

"As a result of these meetings, we only lost one client in the process. And to be honest with you, they were our worst client. The upside is our folks are less stressed out, especially those who had to deal directly with this one problem client.

"Henry, there are two things that I'm really excited about. First, the enthusiasm I see in our staff. Between the coffee bean story and our ability to rally around ACES, we're now functioning like a team, as opposed to a group of individuals doing the best that we can. I now realize that when our employees are excited about work and looking forward the future, success is a natural byproduct.

"Although planning is very important, I now realize that all the planning in the world doesn't make any difference if you don't have a staff committed to executing the plan. The second thing I'm excited about is a recent venture we have underway." Jake went on to explain that over the past several months he and his team had been working diligently to find ways to expand their client base in the energy industry.

They had gone to numerous conferences and set up booths at the associated exhibition halls, all to no avail. At LaserTech's last Senior Management retreat, Colin Jacobs, LaserTech's Chief Technology Officer, had mentioned that he had a college roommate who was working for an engineering consulting firm in Houston. Their families had recently gone on vacation together, and Colin had shared with his friend some of LaserTech's frustrations in marketing to the oil and gas companies.

His friend had invited Colin and Jake to meet with them in their office in Houston and interact with the senior management of the engineering firm.

"I made a brief presentation to the leaders of the consulting firm, explaining to them the basics of our technology. I communicated our belief that our technology could have a real impact on some of the recent failures that were being experienced in the oil field and how our technology was being used in the defense industry to help the military monitor loading on aircraft, tanks, and other equipment.

"As we dialogued with the engineers in the room, it was clear that we had struck a chord with them. The great irony was that this company made their living diagnosing problems, but often struggled collecting the necessary information and data required to make the right decisions and recommendations for their clients.

"Since that time period, we've secured five projects and expect in the next six months to deploy our technology to eight other locations around the world. Not only will we probably increase our business this year by 15%, I expect the engineering firm will also significantly grow their business."

As Henry sat there pondering all that Jake had just relayed to him, he was astounded. Not only in terms of the magnitude of business LaserTech was now doing, but how in such a relatively short period of time Jake and his team had turned things around. "Jake, this is completely amazing. I knew you were good, but not this good."

"No, no, no, Henry. I don't feel that way at all. Actually, I had very little to do with the process. To a large extent, I'm just the mouthpiece for LaserTech. By keeping our staff motivated, focused, and accountable, I have great confidence in our ability to do great things.

"Every day I ask myself if I am making a positive impact on my staff and my family. ACES provides a framework for my assessment, while the beans reminds me that I can make a difference. It sounds so simple, but these concepts have made a huge difference in my life."

Jake and Henry finished lunch and both sat looking out the window at the beautiful golf course. Without saying anything, both men knew that they had significantly impacted each other's lives, in a way that neither of them could have anticipated during their first pizza dinner so many months before.

Before they got up to leave, Henry had a few parting words for his young pupil, "Jake, I can't tell you how much I've enjoyed our time together. Although you probably feel like our time together has been mostly about you and LaserTech, I want you to know how much our time together has meant to me. It has been a long, long time since anyone has been interested in what I knew.

"For years I've felt like an old book placed on a shelf never to be read again. I know at your stage of life this is difficult for you to understand because you always have others placing demands on you, but there will likely come a day when you'll feel as I have felt.

"I'm very proud of you. In the short time you and I have known each other, you've transformed yourself and your company. You should be proud of that. I want to give you something."

Henry reached beneath his chair and pulled a box from inside a bag he had brought. His hands shook as he opened the box. Jake was not sure what to expect and could tell Henry was emotional. "Jake, I planned to give this to one of my sons, but I've decided to give it to you as something to remember me by."

Henry opened the box and slid it across the table to Jake, who could tell it was a medal that Henry had probably received during the war. "Jake, this is *The Distinguished Flying Cross*. It is given to pilots who have served their country, typically in combat. To those of us who came home from the war, it meant a lot; namely that we got to come home in the first place.

"Medals don't mean a whole lot for men who don't come home. Although I know you'll probably never serve as a soldier in war, there is no doubt you've fought battles in your lifetime and will face a few more. My only request is that you keep this medal at your office and when the opportunity presents itself, that you tell others about our time together.

"We need leaders, like you, who are committed to making the world a better place. We need leaders who care about their people and love their families. Between our *Being the Beans* story and ACES, I think you have a message to tell others. I'd like to think that you will impact others around the world, especially with LaserTech's new ventures in the energy industry. Keep on keeping on."

Jake sat in stunned silence for a few minutes. In some regards, he felt completely unworthy to even hold Henry's medal, but he knew Henry wouldn't have given him the medal had he not meant every word that he said. Jake thanked Henry and told him how much he had appreciated everything that Henry had done for him, his family, and his company.

The two men got up to leave and embraced each another. For some strange reason Jake felt like this might be the last time he was going to see Henry. The thought brought tears to his eyes. Henry looked at Jake and said, "Earn this, Jake, earn it." Jake stood there and thought back to his discussion with Henry on *Saving Private Ryan* so many months ago.

Jake was committed to using his time with Henry, and their discussions, to make the world a better place. *Being the beans* was more than just a good story and a neat concept; it was a way to live one's life focused on seeing the world not as it is, but as what it can become.

Although Jake realized there was great power in applying the concept of *Be the Beans* in business, he also knew that there were even greater opportunities in applying this concept to change people's personal lives. Little did he know the impact that a simple decision on his and Lisa's part would have on an entire family for several generations.

SWEET AROMA

Several weeks after his meeting with Henry, Jake asked Lisa about her discussions with Carrie Schneider. Lisa had taken her out to lunch and had been able to get a better handle on the situation. As she had been told, Carrie lost her husband, Steven, to a long bout with cancer. Carrie was truly devastated.

Carrie and Steven had been married for 15 years and had dated since high school. They had both gone to college together in the northeast before moving to Austin, where Steven had worked as a computer programmer.

Although they had done relatively well financially, for some reason Steven had never taken out a life insurance policy before he got sick. Once he was diagnosed with cancer, there was no way to get life insurance. Instead of Carrie going through all of their savings, they had both agreed that when Steven passed away that Carrie would take the children and move in with her parents for a period of time.

Lisa was emotional as she told Jake about her lunch with Carrie. "Jake, I can't even begin to understand what she's going through. It's obvious that Carrie loved Steven very much. She's been devastated by all of this. I told her that you and I were going to help her out. Although she was emotional talking about Steven, she was really emotional once I brought up our helping her."

At Lisa's request, Carrie put together a basic résumé for Jake. She was a college graduate with little work experience as she had decided to stay home with their children. This wouldn't make Jake's job any easier, but he was confident that he could do something for her.

Several weeks later, Jake and Lisa had Carrie and her two children over for dinner. Her son's name was Robert, and her daughter was

Tiffany. As soon as their guests arrived, the Carmichael children took Robert and Tiffany outside to play. All three adults commented on how well the children played together and how easily at that stage of their lives they made friends.

Carrie confided that Robert was really struggling in school. He had become very withdrawn. Tiffany cried a lot, but fortunately she and Carrie were very close.

"Carrie, I'm sure that Lisa told you we'd like to help you, Robert, and Tiffany. I've started making some phone calls, and I believe several of my friends have employment opportunities for you. Along the same lines, we would like to help you out financially. We want you to be honest with us about your needs."

Carrie told Jake and Lisa how much she appreciated their offer to help. Because of pride she struggled with receiving assistance, although she admitted to them that she needed help. She also told them that she sensed the sincerity of their offer and desire to help her family.

Jake called the children in for dinner, and they came storming in the house like a pack of wild dogs. He could tell that Robert and Tiffany were having a good time with their children; a welcome sight for Carrie.

Over the next several months, the Carmichaels and Schneiders spent more time together. Most weekends Robert and Tiffany came over to play. Although Jake and Lisa never communicated very much to their children about the Schneider's situation, Ashley, Anna, and Aaron played an extremely important role in helping build a strong relationship between the two families.

Jake was able to eventually help Carrie find a job working for a friend who needed someone to head his shipping department. Carrie turned out to be a stellar employee. She had excellent organizational skills and was very good at management.

Carrie was also an excellent interface between senior management and the hourly paid staff. Over time, she was promoted to a manager-level position overseeing logistics and operations. Although Carrie was able pay the bills, without the generosity of the Carmichaels she would have struggled financially.

Jake and Lisa purchased a home for Carrie, Robert, and Tiffany three years after their being introduced. Although Carrie frequently commented about how much the Carmichael family had done for her and the children, Jake and Lisa were the first to admit that they were the ones who had been the most impacted.

LaserTech continued to grow and gained a strong reputation in the oil and gas industry as an innovative and high-quality service provider. Jake continued to focus on building strong relationships with his senior leadership and was excited to see their putting ACES to work among their respective teams.

Because of LaserTech's success, Jake was able to spend more time with his family and investing in lives outside of work. This included the time he spent with the Schneiders. He had determined that as a leader the evidence of his success was demonstrated when LaserTech was successful without his direct involvement.

Jake knew how important a father-figure is in the life of a young boy. He and Robert started attending ballgames together. Jake bought Robert a set of golf clubs and started working with him on the fundamentals of the game. Over time, Robert and Jake became very close.

One night when the Schneiders came over for dinner, Jake told Carrie about Henry Schmidt. He had recently passed and Jake was emotional as he shared with Carrie the impact that he had on Jake's life. Jake also told Carrie about the story of *The Beans* and the power it had to transform not only his life, but the life of his company and many of his employees.

Jake also told Carrie that during a trip to Colorado several years ago, he and Lisa had decided they were going to make a concerted effort to have an impact on the life of another family. In some regards Henry's story had influenced that decision. The Schneiders' needs had coincided with that trip. Jake told Carrie that he and Lisa believed it was no accident.

CLOSING SHOP

The Carmichaels and Schneiders remained close friends for many years. As with all families, the children grew up. All of the Carmichael and Schneider children attended college. Jake and Lisa had committed to Carrie that they would provide college educations for Robert and Tiffany. As was so often the case, Carrie was overwhelmed with their generosity. On more than one occasion she told them that she had never known a more generous couple.

After college, Robert moved to the northwest, married, and had children. Tiffany got a job in California, and eventually, Carrie retired. To be closer to her children and grandchildren, Carrie moved to Seattle where Robert lived. Before moving, Jake and Lisa had a going away party for Carrie. All of the Carmichael and Schneider children and their families flew in for the special occasion. There were many tears shed that evening and stories shared during this special gathering.

After everyone left, Carrie sat down with Jake and Lisa. She cried with them in a way that she had not done in many years. "Jake and Lisa, you are the two finest people I've ever known. And odds are, on this side of Heaven you're the two finest people I'll ever know. As I look back over the years, and especially in the lives of Robert and Tiffany, your handprint is all over our lives.

"I marveled tonight as I observed how well-adjusted my children are. I'm quite sure that had you not intervened in our lives, Robert and Tiffany would be very different. Jake, on so many occasions, Robert used to tell me that when he grew up he wanted to be like you—a successful businessman and father. In you, he saw they were both possible. As I look at him today, I think he's on the right path, thanks to you."

Carrie moved to Seattle and enjoyed time with Robert and loved being a grandmother. Living in the same town, she was able to spend many hours with her family and make a tremendous impact on their lives.

Jake served as the president and CEO of LaserTech for a total of 22 years. The company grew and became one of the top technology service providers in the oil and gas industry. Jake and the leaders of the company were approached by an international service firm interested in purchasing LaserTech.

After countless hours of discussions and negotiations, Jake decided to sell LaserTech. After a twelve month transition period where he was retained as president, Jake retired. Although he knew he would miss work, he was looking forward to spending more time with Lisa, traveling, and building relationships with his eight grandchildren.

Several years into their retirement, Jake and Lisa received a letter from Robert. He told them that Carrie had died, but that before she passed away she told him the story of the Beans and that as a family, she had no idea how they could have made it without the Carmichaels. She had also told Robert that Jake and Lisa were the ones who made it possible for him and Tiffany to attend college.

As Jake read the letter, he thought about what a privilege it had been to have such an impact on a hurting family.

Mr. Carmichael,

It has been many years since we have spoken. I still remember the times we used to go to ballgames, play golf, and even that time you took me, Tiffany, and Mom to Disney World. To say you had an impact on my family, and especially me, is an understatement.

This letter is long overdue. The last time we saw each other was the going-away party you had for Mom. She loved your family more than anyone we ever knew. As you know, Mom had to move in with us about 5 years ago. It was not an easy move as she had long enjoyed her independence, but it was clear based on her failing health that living alone was no longer an option.

When she first moved in with us everything seemed fine, but then she started forgetting dates and events from our past. It scared all of us, and we took her to a doctor. The doctor confirmed my suspicion that Mom had Alzheimer's. We are fortunate that her memory loss was very gradual and that for the next several years she really was in pretty good shape.

Our children really loved her, and having her live with us was a wonderful experience. Almost two years to the day after Mom was diagnosed with Alzheimer's, her health really started to deteriorate. She had a hard time remembering our names, and on more than one occasion walked out of the house. She had become a danger to herself and others.

After several months of deliberation, we decided to place her in an assisted care unit. Because she was so confused, she really didn't seem to mind. Within 6 months, she passed away. Watching her struggle was the most difficult experience I have ever undergone. It was even worse than losing Dad.

Before Mom really lost her mental faculties, I had the opportunity to visit with her about some of the more important experiences in her life. Probably the most emotional I have ever seen Mom was when she talked about you and your family.

On more than one occasion, she sobbed uncontrollably when she spoke of you and Mrs. Carmichael. Although I knew that you helped us financially, until I visited with Mom before she really got sick I had no idea all you had done for our family. She was always very guarded when talking about you all, but I guess she knew that she had limited time and that I needed to hear about all you had done for us. I also assumed that you asked her to keep your gifts to our family a secret.

As I write this letter, I'm overwhelmed by what you have done for our family. No telling how I would have turned out. Dad died when I was 11, and I remember being pretty messed up. My whole world had turned upside down. Whether you know it or not, you served as my role model. When I grew up, I wanted to be successful like you and have a wife and family just like you.

I always wondered how Mom paid for college. Whenever I asked she tried to change the subject and said something about a long lost relative setting up a college trust fund for Tiffany and me. I never really thought a lot about it when I was in college, but when I got out something inside of me wanted to know. To Mom's credit, she never cracked until she got sick. She told me that you and Mrs. Carmichael had paid for both my and Tiffany's college—room, board, tuition, and all. Words cannot express how I feel.

My purpose in writing this letter is to extend my deep appreciation for all you have done. I continue to be overwhelmed for all of the goodness you have done. I hope that at some point I can do one-tenth for someone what you have done for me. I'm not sure what would have happened to us had you not intervened.

Our world would be a much better place if all successful business people were like you. Although I am sure the money you gave to our family could have been invested and grown, I would like to think that your investment in Mom, Tiffany, and me is worth more than any mutual fund could ever provide. It's a shame that we don't see helping people as investments, isn't it? My guess is that you figured this out a long time ago.

When I was a kid, Mom also told me the story about the coffee beans. I have told that story to countless individuals over the years, and it was a common reference used by Mom for motivating me.

Thank you again for all you've done. I hope at some point to see you again and bring my family. My wife and children have heard many stories about the Carmichaels, and I imagine that they feel as if they already know you. Please pass my regards onto Mrs. Carmichael and convey to her the deep appreciation that our family has for you both.

With deepest appreciation,
Robert Schneider

Lisa watched Jake read the letter and could see tears in his eyes. "Honey, are you ok?" she asked.

Jake had to pause for a moment to collect his thoughts before responding to Lisa. "I just received a letter from Robert Schneider, Carrie's son. She passed away last month. He wrote to tell me that she had told him what we had done for them and was writing to tell us thank you.

"It's been a long time since I've thought about that family. There were times when I wondered if we were doing the right thing, but in reading this letter there is no doubt we made the right decision."

As Jake pondered the Schneider family and the decision that he and Lisa had made so many years ago to help them, he couldn't help but think about Henry. Jake could almost hear Henry telling him to *be the beans* and make a difference in the world.

Jake felt a sense of honor in realizing that he and Lisa had used their resources to make the world a better place. Even better, Jake knew that because of what he had done for others, the actions of his life were impacting people he would never meet or know. This to him was the real definition of success and purpose in life.

EPILOGUE

For most of us, it's possible to identify individuals who have *been the beans* in our lives. These are people who have the ability to rise above their circumstances and not "let the turkeys get them down", as my father used to say.

Along the same lines, we also know people who always seem to see the worst in every situation, the "half-empty" crowd. My wife and I were in Disney World a few years ago and we saw a T-shirt that says it all for the "half-emptys" in our lives, *I'm Grumpy Because You're Dopey.*

To a large extent, the world seeks to pull us down both physically and emotionally. If you are alive long enough, you can definitely sense it in your own life, career, and family. It is easy to succumb and just give in to the pressure to conform.

If you ask most recent high school and college graduates about their hopes and dreams, their ideas are almost limitless. With great confidence they speak of grand aspirations and desires to make the world a better place. At times, their views are almost comical to the "seasoned veterans of life", but there is also great comfort in knowing that some of us still have the ability to dream.

After high school and college at some point over the next twenty or so years, our youthful enthusiasm and optimism begin to wane. The deep-seated convictions and plans that were so confidently pursued in our youth are replaced with reality and what one might call *a more subdued sense of life's purpose*. In all honesty, it's just plain sad that life does this to us. Why does life have to be this way?

The answer to this most profound question is at the core of Teddy Roosevelt's "Citizenship in a Republic" speech at Sorbonne, Paris on

April 23, 1910. The quote is often referred to as the "Man in the Arena" speech, and it is one of my favorite quotes.

> It is not the critic who counts: not the man who points out how the strong man stumbles or where the doer of deeds could have done better. The credit belongs to the man who is actually in the arena, whose face is marred by dust and sweat and blood, who strives valiantly, who errs and comes up short again and again, because there is no effort without error or shortcoming, but who knows the great enthusiasms, the great devotions, who spends himself for a worthy cause; who, at the best, knows, in the end, the triumph of high achievement, and who, at the worst, if he fails, at least he fails while daring greatly, so that his place shall never be with those cold and timid souls who knew neither victory nor defeat.

The "voice of the critic" brings a crushing blow to the heart of the dreamer. As John F. Kennedy once said, "We need men who can dream of things that never were." **Without dreams nothing happens, literally nothing.** When I speak of dreams, I am not talking about fanciful wishes based on *delusions of grandeur*, but the idea that each of us can make a contribution to the world around us.

The setting for this book is focused on business, so the idea would be that you dream about the opportunity to make a meaningful impact on the people you work with and the business that employs you. Who doesn't want this in life? However, the concept of making the world a better place obviously extends to our ability to impact organizations like families, friends, churches, schools, and non-profits.

How do we deal with the critic, or those with a critical spirit, who do the most damage to those who want to make an impact, or might we say—*be the beans*? There are at least three options. The first is to ignore them. To be heard, one must have an audience. If you ignore the voice of the critic, at least in your own mind they will be silenced.

The second is to try and win them over to your view. This option is certainly not easy, but as conveyed in the idea of the coffee bean changing its environment, you must determine to be a source of change and not a passive-responder to a caustic environment.

The third option and the one only likely if you are in a position of authority, is to fire the negative person or persons. One of my favorite websites is despair.com where they comment, "Sometimes the best solution to morale problems is just to fire all of the unhappy people".

Obviously, this is a last resort, but as Jim Collins conveyed in his book, *Good to Great*, to be successful as an organization you must get the right people on the bus and the wrong people off the bus.

In spite of the odds, there are a few brave souls who weather the storms of life and against all odds, they maintain that sense of undying optimism that is at the heart of every dreamer and successful organization. For you and me, the question is how do we capture in our own lives what seems to be innate for those who are naturally gifted with this ability?

To use an analogy from golf, we must study what makes the professional golfer's swing work and attempt to mimic it in our own swing. Having a positive view of the world certainly comes easier for some than others, but as Abraham Lincoln once said, "Most folks are about as happy as they make up their minds to be."

After I left college, I became a better student of those who seemed to have the greatest impact on the world around them because of their positive outward image. Growing up, I certainly saw this modeled wonderfully in my parents, Judy and Richard Alexander. Today, I also see it being lived out in the life of my brother, Jonathan, who is a pastor in Seattle, Washington.

In the closing section of this book, I would like to identify three individuals who could proudly wear a "Be the Beans" T-shirt. It is easy to talk about being a positive influence on the world and what it should look like, but the real challenge is to do it.

What makes the three following individuals unique is that in a real sense they are different because they have chosen to not be like most people in the world. *Like the negative person who can choose to be happy, the optimist can choose to be a pessimist.*

People who have a positive outward view of life have learned to focus more on what is good, and less on what is bad. They have learned to "major in the majors and minor in the minors" (one of my father's favorite sayings).

As you read about the three following individuals, consider two items. First, who are the individuals in your life who have had the greatest impact on you and maintained that uncommon sense of optimism, regardless of their circumstances?

Secondly, as you think about your life, would those around you describe you as someone who has impacted their life in a positive way? If the answer is "yes", consider what you are doing correctly, and keep on keeping on! If you struggle to answer this second question, what are some specific steps you can take to be more intentional in impacting those around you? If all else fails, ask those around you what you can do to improve.

Joe Fowler, President of
Stress Engineering Services, Inc.

I first met Joe in March 1993 during my interview with Stress Engineering Services, Inc. (my current employer) in Houston, Texas. Over the past almost 20 years, I have witnessed this engineering consulting company grow from roughly 40 people to more than 400 people, serving almost 1,000 clients around the world. Stress Engineering is a wonderful company with one of the greatest positive cultures in the world, built on technical excellence combined with a spirit of service and cooperation.

The very heartbeat of this culture is company president and co-founder, Joe Fowler. For more than 40 years, Joe has been the driving force in the growth of Stress Engineering. He literally lights up a room when he walks in and is recognized around the world for his gracious spirit, generosity, and commitment to helping people achieve their dreams.

It has been my observation that great companies have great leaders who inspire their employees to achieve great things. For the past four decades, Joe has been doing this by inspiring others to make the most of opportunities.

One of the most profound observations I have made about Joe is his ability to see the best in others, regardless of the circumstances or what they might have done. The same could be true in his ability to observe the best in "less than ideal" situations. A lot of people struggle with this particular issue in terms of seeing the best in others and situations. Ultimately, it limits their success and ability to impact others.

Some people are great leaders, while others go the next step in developing great leaders. From my perspective, leaders who develop leaders are those individuals who leave a lasting mark on the world around them. I once heard it said that *the quality of your leadership is defined more by what happens in your absence than in your presence.* Joe Fowler is the embodiment of this principle, as reflected in his being a leader of leaders.

Fred Wilson, President of Armor Plate, Inc.

I met Fred Wilson in January of 1998. Over the past 15 years I have had the unique privilege of serving Fred as a consultant and also traveling with him around the world (I recently coined these excursions *Field Trips with Fred*). The bottom line is that Fred Wilson is just plain funny, always keeps you laughing, and has an undying sense of optimism.

While in China in 2005, I witnessed on multiple occasions Fred making an entire room of Chinese engineers laugh, even though Fred spoke no Chinese and most of the people in the room did not speak English (now that's just plain incredible!). He has a story for every occasion and probably has 100 or more witty quotes he can throw into any conversation on the fly.

Two of my favorite quotes from Fred's are: *It all depends on whose ox is getting gored* and *Opportunity never looks nearly as big as it does in the rearview mirror.* Fred runs a small business that employs 25-30 people. What many Americans do not understand is that to run a business, especially in today's anti-business climate that imposes high taxes and excessive regulations, is patently tough.

Business owners like Fred are under a lot of pressure and responsibility to serve not only their employees, but the families of their employees. Owners like Fred will pay their employees before they pay themselves. Yet through all of these challenges, Fred always has an upbeat spirit.

Fred has impacted me in so many ways, but there are two specific ways that come to mind. The first is his positive outlook on life (the obvious reason he is mentioned in this section of the book). He has the ability to see the best in situations and maintain a positive outlook towards the future, *regardless of the circumstances.*

The second way Fred has impacted me is by instilling in me a love for business and being an entrepreneur. The '*Be the beans*' barometer "maxes out" when others seek what we do because of the positive impact that we have on their lives. Fred has this quality in spades. If you have others around you, especially those you lead, who want to emulate what you do, you are having a meaningful impact on the world around you.

Tanya Alexander, My Wife

I wonder how many husbands would put their wives down as a *Be the Beans* kind of person? Marriage has a way of being the true crucible for bringing out the best and the worst in all of us. My wife, Tanya, has for the past 20 years not only put up with me, but also demonstrated to me how much fun one can have in leading others.

When we first met, I described Tanya as a beautiful, bubbly, blonde cheerleader. However, as I fell in love with her I realized there was something very unique about her; primarily, her ability to always see the best in others and the best in the situations of life.

While Tanya and I were dating, my parents fell in love with her (confirmation for me that I needed to marry her!). She and I started dating my junior year in college. Because in college I lived in the same town where I grew up, my parents had hundreds of opportunities to spend time with Tanya before we were even engaged.

There are at least two stories that remind me of how my parents loved Tanya. Like all good parents, they wanted the best for me. I decided to ask Tanya to marry me during the fall of my senior year. I remember discussing this with my parents as I planned to go to graduate school the following year. This meant that Tanya and I would be married while we were both in school (my being in graduate school while Tanya completed her Bachelor's degree).

There were the usual discussions with my parents about money and responsibility, but the comment I remember most came from my father. "Bubba (yes, I'm from Texas, and that's my nickname at home), you better hope Tanya says 'yes', because if she says 'no' you better look for another family. We're going to keep her!" I have no doubt that he was serious in making this statement. Fortunately for me, she said "yes".

The second story came the next January before I proposed to Tanya. She went snow skiing with my family during the Christmas break. My father and I were riding up one of the chair lifts at Keystone in Colorado. I will never forget one of the conversations that we had.

He looked over at me and said, "Bubba, don't you ruin her; don't you make her like you." We both laughed, but I knew exactly what he meant. Although I am happy most of the time, like a lot of folks, I can be a grump when things don't go my way. Tanya is not this way and frankly, it's difficult for me to understand. She is the most even-keeled person I have ever known. She does not let things get her down, but always seems to find joy, even in the midst of the storms of life.

I have done my best to heed my father's advice, although I know my influence on Tanya has at times been *less than stellar*. In all honesty, for the past 20 years I have tried to be *less like me and more like Tanya* in terms of how I view the world and how I treat those around me. I am not sure there is a better compliment one could make about another person, especially someone to whom they are married!

ACKNOWLEDGEMENTS

This book went through several iterations before the final version resulted. Several of my colleagues at Stress Engineering took time to read the original draft and their feedback is very much appreciated. The first-round reviewers included Richard Biel, Julian Bedoya, Wendy Courtright, Rhett Dotson, Greg Garic, Ron Scrivner, Brent Vyvial, and Bobby Wright.

The development of the appendices was suggested by Brent Vyvial, while the addition of the Schneiders was based on Ron Scrivner's recommendation to broaden the appeal of the book to a wider audience. Greg Garic, true to form as a detailed engineer, had several pages of suggestions for me that contributed significantly to the final version of the book.

It is wonderful to work with a group of friends who care enough to provide constructive feedback (and not be afraid to share their opinions!).

Other reviewers included Dean Unsicker, Head of School at Rosehill Christian School, and my best friend from high school, Morgan Cassady, Vice President at CIS Group, LLC.

I would also like to thank Evalyn Shea, Leslie Mohr, and Jordan Flippin of Shea Writing and Training Solutions, Inc. Jordan played a critical role in reviewing the text and her suggestions are very much appreciated.

Finally, I am deeply indebted to Nicole Soltis for her permission to use stories told by her grandfather, Mr. Ted Conlin; the World War II fighter pilot who served as the inspiration for Henry Schmidt.

IN MEMORY OF A REAL HERO

Although Henry Schmidt is a fictitious character, the real-life hero who served as the inspiration for our hero was P-51 pilot, Raymond "Ted" Conlin. Mr. Conlin passed away on March 12, 2012 at the age of 91.[1] His passing occurred approximately one month after I started writing this book. Unfortunately I never had the opportunity to meet him.

I found Mr. Conlin and learned about his life through various searches on the Internet, which started in February 2012 with a Google search of "P-51 pilots" that directed me to the website of Paul and Sue Liles[2]. As a World War II fighter pilot, Mr. Conlin flew 71 missions, logging 270 combat hours I. He participated in many of the major Allied offensives in the liberation of occupied Europe, including D-Day. He was awarded the Air Medal with 4 Clusters, 4 major Battle Stars, and the Russian Medal of Great Patriotic War.

Mr. Conlin returned from World War II and married Audrey, his wife of 64 years. They met during the war when he was stationed in England. The couple moved to Long Beach and bought a house in Los Altos. In 1950 he took his GED and enrolled at USC, earning a B.S. degree in Business. He owned his own insurance brokerage firm and retired from the business in 1985.

Mr. Conlin was a regular at Old Ranch Country Club and was among the first to join the club in the mid-1960s. He was a lifelong regular at the club, playing golf, backgammon and gin rummy. Provided on the following page are two photos of him. Pictures are indeed worth a thousand words.

---

[1]   Excerpts from Mr. Conlin's obituary by Tim Grobaty, published in the *Long Beach Press-Telegram* on March 19, 2012.

[2]   http://www.lilesnet.com/conlin/stories/index.htm

APPENDICES

OVERVIEW OF THE APPENDICES

These appendices have been prepared to provide the reader with resources for more effectively putting the concepts presented in this story to work. The addition of these appendices is based on feedback from several initial readers who believed value would be added to the book in having additional resources.

Readers are also encouraged to visit our website, www.bethebeans. com for additional ideas for making your impact on the world, and also finding out what others who have read the book are doing to *Be the Beans*.

In many regards, these appendices are written as if you and I are sitting down together over a cup of coffee. Much of the contents is based on my experiences and seeing what works and what does not. Feel the freedom to build on what is presenting by adding your own style. As I often comment to my colleagues, "We all have the right to get better".

Appendix A provides practical ways that the ACES concepts of accountability, commitment, excellence, and service can be applied to practically any organization.

Appendix B includes a *Small Group Discussion Sheet* that can be used by team leaders to facilitate discussions for putting the concepts for success presented in this book to work for your company, church, or organization.

APPENDIX A—THE ACES DEVELOPMENT PROCESS

As Henry communicated to Jake, the story of the *Carrot, Egg, and Coffee Beans* is a wonderful story to remind us that *our outlook on the world often determines the impact that we have*. When we have a positive outlook on the world, we are far more likely to see challenges as speed bumps rather than treacherous mountains that cannot be conquered.

The real value in a story is its ability to shape our lives. For those of us in business, the bottom line is how we use the motivation behind a story to *expand our territories*. The purpose of this appendix is to provide you with a resource for putting ACES to work for you and your company. The key is to create a culture built around the characteristics embodied in ACES—Accountability, Commitment, Excellence, and Service. The key is not to create a system of checklists. <u>Cultures endure and transcend time; checklists are easy to forget and do little to foster long-term success.</u>

Provided below is the ACES graphic, along with highlights of what Henry said to describe the concept behind ACES to Jake.

Accountability
Set clear expectations

Commitment
Carry out the mission at all costs

Excellence
DO over SHOW ratio > 1

Service
Expectations + 1

Thoughts from Henry

Accountability is what keeps us honest. Knowing that others are depending on us motivates us to do our best. Along the same lines, we must give people permission to kick us in the rear when we fall short. Accountability is the glue that holds every organization together. As a leader, your job is to create a culture where the members of your team are accountable to you and one another. No one is an island, and our actions always have consequences that impact others. There is way too much focus on individuality in the world. Successful people and teams realize that they need other people. Make sure your people know their responsibilities, and that they know they will be held accountable to do their job well. Give others permission to hold you accountable as well. It goes a long way to building trust, which is essential for a strong culture.

Commitment is built on trust and mutual cooperation. Look at any great company, team, or organization, and I guarantee that you will find a high level of commitment among the individuals within that organization. We are all committed to a lot of things, but organizations must be committed to a mission, which obviously implies that you have one. If you do not have a well-defined mission statement, one that everyone understands—you better get one. Everyone in your organization must have a deep-seated commitment to your mission, your organization's purpose, which drives everything you do.

Excellence. Excellence does not mean that you have to be better than everyone else; it just means you have to do your best. Woody Allen once said that 90% of success was just showing up. As a leader, you need to challenge your people to be excellent. This is your number one job as you challenge them to be the best they can with the skills and resources they have been given. All successful organizations are good at something, but to be the best you have to be excellent at what you do. In today's competitive market excellence is what distinguishes you from your competition—and equally important—it's what keeps your clients coming back and telling others about you.

Service. At the core of this word is *serve*. To serve means that you put the needs of others before yourself. Good service is so rare today that when we experience it, we recognize it almost immediately because it stands out from most of the service we get. People might forget what you say or do, but they'll never forget how you make them feel. As a leader, your attitude should be that you *lead so that you may serve*. There are very few leaders who do this. Most people see servant-leadership as a weakness, but history has shown that to be wrong. George Washington and Abraham Lincoln embodied what it meant to be servant-leaders, and a lot of people, then and now, loved them for it. We need more servant leaders in our world today.

Putting ACES to work

Odds are that if you have a group that has been operating for any period of time, you already have some of the ACES characteristics at work. Even a somewhat dysfunctional team has to have at least some elements of accountability, commitment, excellence, or service going for it!

Remember that the goal is to create a *culture of ACES*. Oftentimes, the hardest part of any organizational change is getting started. Provided below are the four ACES characteristics, along with a basic framework for how to create and execute activities that support each characteristic. Don't go crazy as you start this process. Introduce ACES as if you are eating an elephant, *slowly*—one bite at a time.

Accountability

Of all four characteristics, accountability is probably the most important element for building a team. Embodied in accountability is the idea that <u>we know what is expected of us and that we are going to be held accountable</u>. One of the fundamental mistakes made by many leaders is failure to communicate what is expected of their subordinates.

Failure to communicate leads to confusion and disharmony. How can we as leaders create a *culture of accountability* for those placed under our charge? Listed below are some of the ways that leaders can foster a *culture of accountability* on their teams.

- If accountability is applied at the group level, meet with your team for an "Accountability Kick-Off" meeting. During this meeting, identify areas of accountability. These typically involve tasks that must be completed by individual team members. To increase the likelihood for success, assign specific personnel to each identified task, and designate a target completion date. <u>Defined goals and target completion dates are the building blocks for accountability.</u>

- When your team accomplishes a goal, provide a reward. The reward can either be determined at the time of the goal setting or it can be a surprise at the time of completion. If you own the company or have direct control over bonuses, financial incentives are powerful. However, if you do not have direct influence in the financial rewarding of your team, you need to look for other options.[3] Listed below are several ideas for you to consider. The last two items can also be part of an ongoing program to show appreciation to staff members throughout the year (strongly encouraged).
  - o Dinner at a nice restaurant with your staff and their spouses.
  - o Take your team to a college or professional sporting event.
  - o Hunting or fishing trips with your team.
  - o Gift cards to restaurants and sporting-goods stores.
  - o Cards for your staff on their birthdays and anniversary employment dates.
  - o Parties at your house for your staff and their spouses. (We have an annual Christmas party that is an extremely important part of our team. We enjoy being together, and it shows.)

- For accountability to work there must be follow-up. Your staff needs to know that after you have set goals and a timeframe for completion, you are going to ask them about it. Like good parenting, <u>consistency is the key</u>. Consider the Annual Accountability Calendar provided in Table A1.

Provided in Table A1 is an example Annual Accountability Calendar. This resource was developed for our team to ensure that during the course of a year we would accomplish what we set out to

---

[3] One of the best books on employee incentives is *The Carrot Principle: How the Best Managers Use Recognition to Engage Their Employees, Retain Talent, and Drive Performance* by Adrian Gostick and Chester Elton. Keeping employees motivated is essential for leaders who care about their staff and want to accomplish the most with their teams.

do and revisit critical plans for building our business. The contents of the event calendar are not nearly as important as getting your specific goals and objectives down on paper. These goals should be revisited at every meeting. Time should be allocated during each meeting for what was to be completed in the prior month and what is to be completed in the coming month.

Table A1—Annual Accountability Calendar

Month	Activity	Comments and Notes
January	S.W.O.T. Assessment [1] Strength	Weakness	Opportunity	Threat	
February	Gap Analysis[2]	
March	Review of *Goals and Objectives* Identify potential workshops to host	
April	Personnel Review & Individual Goal Setting / Update CVs	Be sure to integrate ACES
May	Review of Marketing Materials Evaluate JIP opportunities	
June	Conferences & Papers (inventory)[3] Identify and updated paper topics listing	
July	Strategy Session: *Seven-Step Strategic Initiative Process*	
August	Discuss the Seven-Step opportunities and review *individual goals* from April	
September	Identify conferences to attend Discuss techniques for attending conferences Make a client Christmas gift list	Get conferences on the group calendar
October	Annual Group Retreat	Read a selected book (preferably one with an assessment test)
November	Focus on *Client Service* Send client Christmas gifts Identify key companies and contacts How can we better serve our clients?	
December	Year-end summary assessment Review paper topics listing from June	Review S.W.O.T.

Notes for Table A1:

1. The S.W.O.T. analysis is an assessment of the strengths, weaknesses, opportunities, and threats associated with your company. It is an excellent means for evaluating the capabilities of your organization, as well as the external elements like competition and opportunities in the marketplace.

2. The *Gap Analysis* is a follow-up activity to evaluate STRENGTHS to minimize THREATS and leverage OPPORTUNITIES to offset WEAKNESSES.

3. In some industries (e.g. oil and gas industries), conferences play an important role in marketing services, disseminating knowledge, and networking. Presenting technical papers is an excellent means for building credibility and enhancing business connections. One of the best discussions on this subject comes from Ford Harding in his book, *Rain Making: The Professional's Guide to Attracting New Clients* (specifically, Chapter 2: Finding a Podium).

Commitment

In discussing *Accountability*, we identified means for creating a culture where a team or business is motivated and challenged to accomplish goals and objectives; however, *Commitment* is the key to making it happen. As Thomas Edison said, *Vision without execution is hallucination*. People can accomplish a great deal when they are committed to an <u>idea</u>, but they can go to even greater lengths when they are committed to other <u>people</u>.

To create a *culture of commitment*, leaders must strive to build teams where each member understands the role that they play and members are encouraged to do their best to support the team using the skills and talents that they have. Listed below are some of the ways that leaders can foster a *culture of commitment* on their teams.

- Develop a well-defined mission statement. If possible, integrate your team in developing the mission statement. *Involvement precedes commitment* are great words to live by for leaders seeking to build consensus.
- Commitment must exist at all levels of the organization. Everyone in your organization must have a deep-seated commitment to your mission.
- We are all committed to a lot of things, but successful organizations must have a central point of focus. An excellent point of focus is to challenge employees to provide high-quality customer service. I joked several years ago that our motto should be, *We are so committed, we should be committed*.
- Commitment is built on trust and mutual cooperation. Top-notch sports teams and elite military units like the Army Rangers and Navy Seals are excellent examples of trust at work. In your effort to create a culture of commitment, remember that trust is the glue that hold it all together.

Excellence

As simple as it sounds, excellence is knowing what you are doing and consistently doing it. If you are in business, your clients are paying you because they assume you know what you are doing and that you can deliver the goods and services you have promised.

Most of us are on a short leash with clients, who often remind us that we are only as good as our last job. Although many of us are price conscious, we all know that *you get what you pay for.* In some situations the importance of quality and excellence is so important, that price is not even considered. One of the best examples in our country today concerns surgeons. If someone close to you requires emergency brain surgery, you are not likely to get on the Internet and look for the low-cost provider. The most successful businesses never abuse customers or over-charge for their services; however, they realize that to provide excellence, there is a price that must be paid.

Listed below are some of the ways that leaders can foster a *culture of excellence* on their teams:

- As a leader, have a reputation for excellence. It is hard to expect excellence from others if you have not demonstrated this characteristic in your own life.
- Encourage those on your team to develop skills to enhance their capabilities. As your staff improves, so does your team. This includes encouraging them to attend short courses and allowing the opportunity to pursue additional education if it will benefit your team and/or company.
- *Inspect for excellence.* This is similar to the elements addressed in the Accountability discussion. Remember the old saying, *you get what you inspect, not what you expect.* As your staff grows, new employees will quickly learn the importance of excellence if it is already built into your culture.
- Be in the business of *exceeding expectations.* As a friend of mine often says, make sure that your SHOW over DO ratio is greater than one. Don't talk about doing something if you can't deliver.

Service

Service is the part of your business that people can touch and feel. I remember years ago hearing something that has stuck with me—*People might forget what you say, but they'll never forget how you make them feel.* People might not necessarily hire you or buy your goods because of your service, but rest assured—if they experience good service, they will keep coming back.

Let's admit it, providing good service can be exhausting, especially as your business grows. Listed below are a few suggestions for ways that leaders can foster a *culture of service* on their teams:

- Recognize when members of your team provide top-notch service. This will not only be an encouragement to them, but will also set a tone for your team that you value providing high-quality service.
- Don't be afraid to survey your customers to find out what they think about the service you are offering. I <u>do not recommend</u> that you make this a major focus of your business because it can become a distraction in and of itself; however, it is important to know what your customers think so that you can make adjustments if necessary.
- While most of your clients will have reasonable expectations of the services you offer, there will always be a few who want something for nothing. In a polite way, tell these customers that you will be happy to address their concerns, but *their expectations need to be commensurate with your compensation.* Remember that no matter how hard you try, you cannot please everyone.
- Take time to learn what your customers want. Take them to lunch, a ballgame, or play golf—something other than a phone call or e-mail (heck, telemarketers can do that!). Not only will the extra gesture let your customers know that you value them personally and want to spend time with them, but when your service might not be everything it could be, they are willing to give you the benefit of the doubt.

APPENDIX B—SMALL GROUP DISCUSSION SHEET

1. The reason that the story of the *Carrot, Egg, and Coffee Beans* resonates with so many of us is that there are times when we get down emotionally. Over the past 6 months, what are some things that have gotten you down emotionally?
2. Of the items identified in Question #1, what are the sources of your personal frustration? Common sources include inter-personal relationship issues, lost opportunities, and failures.
3. Some have noted that many of the frustrations in our lives stem from *unfulfilled expectations*. As you look back over your responses to Questions #1 and #2, would you say that the <u>issue of unfulfilled expectations</u> is at the root of some frustrations in your life? If this is the case, how could managing expectations help you better deal with the challenges in your life (i.e. *Be the beans*)?
4. During Jake's interaction with Henry in applying the *Carrot, Egg, and Coffee Beans,* Jake is challenged to apply the concept of ACES to his personal life and company. Next to each of the following ACES characteristics, explain what each means to you. In developing your answer, think in terms of how your positive contribution can impact your organization's overall success (i.e., business, church, group, etc.).

Accountability:

Commitment:

Excellence:

Service:

5. What are some practical ways that you can put ACES to work for you both personally and in business? Review the contents provided in Appendix A for additional insights.
6. Most of us realize how important it is to be involved in the lives of others. A main element in *Be the Beans* centers on investing in people.
    a. Identify people who have been brought into your life who could benefit from an investment on your part.
    b. Make a list of specific steps can you take to impact those people identified in (a). <u>Remember that one person can make a significant difference.</u>

ABOUT THE AUTHOR

Chris Alexander is an eternal optimist and believes that one person can make a significant difference in the lives of others. As a Christian, he is challenged on a daily basis that living for Christ is the ultimate way to *Be the Beans*.

Chris is a Principal at Stress Engineering Services, Inc. in Houston, Texas. In addition to being a registered professional mechanical engineer with degrees from Texas A&M University, he has also spent much of his career in business development and management. His great passion is to help others identify their purpose in life and encourage them to become what they have been called to be.

Chris lives north of Houston in Magnolia with his wife, Tanya, and their three children.

CPSIA information can be obtained at www.ICGtesting.com
Printed in the USA
LVOW051356150213

320072LV00003B/10/P